EXPLORING THE
BASICS OF THE BIBLE

Other Evangelical Training Association books from
Crossway Books

Exploring the Old Testament
Exploring the New Testament
Exploring Church History

EXPLORING THE

BASICS

OF THE BIBLE

R. Laird Harris, Ph.D.

CROSSWAY BOOKS

A DIVISION OF
GOOD NEWS PUBLISHERS
WHEATON, ILLINOIS

Exploring the Basics of the Bible

Copyright © 2002 by Evangelical Training Association

Published by Crossway Books
      a division of Good News Publishers
      1300 Crescent Street
      Wheaton, Illinois 60187

Previously published by Evangelical Training Association, copyright © 1990.

Unless noted otherwise, Scripture quotations are taken from the *Holy Bible, King James Version.*

Scripture taken from the *Holy Bible: New International Version®* is identified NIV. Copyright © 1973, 1978, 1984 by International Bible Society. Used by permission of Zondervan Publishing House. All rights reserved.

The "NIV" and "New International Version" trademarks are registered in the United States Patent and Trademark Office by International Bible Society. Use of either trademark requires the permission of International Bible Society.

Scripture quotations marked NASB are taken from the *New American Standard Bible®* Copyright © The Lockman Foundation 1960, 1962, 1963, 1968, 1971, 1972, 1973, 1975, 1977, 1995. Used by permission. (www.Lockman.org)

Cover design: Cindy Kiple

First printing 2002

Printed in the United States of America

Library of Congress Cataloging-in-Publication Data
Harris, R. Laird (Robert Laird), 1911-
  Exploring the basics of the Bible / R. Laird Harris.
    p. cm.
  Previously published: Evangelical Training Association, c1990.
  Includes bibliographical references.
  ISBN 1-58134-370-1 (pbk. : alk. paper)
  1. Bible—Introductions. I. Title.
BS475.3 .H37   2002
220.6'1—dc21   2001005822
                                CIP

15	14	13	12	11	10	09	08	07	06	05	04	03	02
15	14	13	12	11	10	9	8	7	6	5	4	3	2	1

CONTENTS

REVELATION AND INSPIRATION

The Book of Genesis records how God created mankind in His own image and likeness. One of God's purposes was that Adam should have contact and communion with Him. It is clear from the account that God did care for Adam, talk with him, and give him commands. For the most high God to speak with people in this way was a wonderful revelation of God's word, His being, and His will.

After the sin of Adam and Eve, God could indeed have cast them off. They had deliberately disobeyed; the threat had been death. But God in boundless mercy interposed a divinely intended plan of salvation. So God sought out Adam in the garden and charged him with his sin. This was God's first revelation to fallen man.

SPECIAL AND GENERAL REVELATION

God spoke further with Adam, Eve, the serpent, Cain, Noah, and many others. This direct communication from God is usually called special revelation.

Much can be learned about God from the universe He has made. Such an enormous creation signifies an almighty God. The marvelous intricacy of the world argues for the infinite wisdom of God. Our consciences testify to us of a holy and benevolent God. These evidences of God in His creation are usually called general revelation.

This general revelation has often been denied. People say that what seems to be intricacy in nature is due to chance, and the "moral law within," called conscience, has been ascribed to society, early training, self-deception, etc. But Paul in Romans 1:19-23 clearly affirms that God can be seen in nature, and he clearly refers to conscience in Romans 2:15. Actually, it is an impressive phenomenon that the great majority of people have always believed in some kind of deity. Furthermore, although conscience can be denied, every known human culture has some moral rules. It would seem that natural revelation is well established. That it does not lead people to worship the true God is attributed by Paul to human wickedness (Rom. 1:18).

INSPIRATION

When God spoke to people in the early times, it was an oral special revelation. As far as we know, there was no writing until some time after the Flood. Some method of recording numbers of objects may have been used, but it seems that writing as we know it began in Mesopotamia and Egypt a little before 3000 B.C. God's oral revelation, however, was just as special and true and inspired as His later written words. When God spoke to Cain, it was not the voice of conscience within; Cain answered in anger. It was an objective speaking from God.

No one knows the names of many of the people to whom God spoke in the early days. Although the Old Testament records that Enoch "walked with God," the word here probably refers to habitual living rather than mere walking together. But in any case, it indicates a harmony and a fellowship including discourse. This fits with the New Testament reference to Enoch as a prophet (Jude 14). Noah received extensive revelations from God—even as to the dimensions of the ark, the animals to be assembled, etc. Without these specific revelations Noah would have perished too. He did not get the instructions for the ark from his heightened spiritual imagination.

A further lesson from Noah's life is that he ministered the word of God to his generation. The record in Genesis implies and 2 Peter states that Noah warned his generation of the coming judgment. This is the function of a prophet—having received the word of God, to speak it to the people.

While the Bible contains no information on God's revelation during the long years from Noah to Abraham, it says much after that. God spoke to Abraham many times. He gave him specific commands and promises that were fulfilled in ways Abraham could not have guessed. Abraham moved in society as a prince (Gen. 23:5) and as a worshiper of the true God (Gen. 14:22). By life and word he ministered to his generation, and through the record Moses wrote, he ministers also to us.

Moses was the first writing prophet. God spoke to Moses face to face (Num. 12:8). In addition, God ordered Moses to write His commands (Exod. 24:4-8). Most of the Pentateuch after Moses' call in Exodus 2 is governed by such expressions as "the Lord said to Moses." At the end of Deuteronomy, it says that Moses wrote down this law of the

Lord and instructed the people to obey its commands and to read it publicly at the Feast of Tabernacles every seven years (Deut. 31:9-13).

More will be said about the prophets and their work in chapter 4. For now, we shall study some of the consequences of this view of the Old Testament prophets as organs of revelation, God's spokesmen to the people (Exod. 7:1-2). Remember that a prophet in Israel was not just a highly spiritual man. A prophet was a man called of God to receive revelation from Him (Num. 12:2-8). The prophet's word was so much God's word that it was as if the prophet had eaten a scroll from heaven and had given it out orally to the people (Ezek. 2:7—3:3). The word spoken was God's word.

The same must be said of the words the prophets wrote. All prophetic messages were not written down. Uriah prophesied in the name of the Lord as Jeremiah had done, but he was killed by King Jehoiakim, and his words were not written (Jer. 26:20-21). But when the Lord spoke through the prophets in ancient Israel, their words were truly God's word, whether they were merely spoken or also written down. Joshua wrote his record in the Book of the Law of God (Josh. 24:26). Much, if not most, of the Old Testament was spoken first and written afterwards.

Some make a distinction between the prophetic speech and the prophetic writing, saying that only the writing was inspired, but the Old Testament makes no such distinction.

These examples illustrate what is meant by the term "inspiration of the Scriptures." A good definition is "that work of the Holy Spirit in chosen individuals by which the person is moved to speak or write in his own idiom the very words of God without error in fact, doctrine, or judgment." Chapters 2 and 3 will give further biblical evidence for this concept.

VERBAL INSPIRATION

This view of inspiration holds that the words themselves are truly God's words, inspired by the Holy Spirit. It is sometimes caricatured as a "dictation theory." But most conservatives today do not believe that God simply dictated His Word to scribes working like a modern secretary or a robot. God used the prophets and controlled them, but He did not violate their styles or personalities. The nearest thing to a theory of dictation is the teaching of the Roman Catholic Council of Trent in 1545, which said in Latin that the Scriptures were "*Spiritu Sancto dictante.*" But the Latin *dictante* does not mean "dictate" in the modern sense. It simply means "spoken" or "said."

INFALLIBLE AND INERRANT

Historically, the Bible has been called inspired, meaning that it is God's Word and fully true. Traditionally, it was also called infallible. That is to say, it is incapable of mistake. In more recent times conservative believers have considered belief in the Bible as "the only infallible rule of faith and life." They clearly meant to affirm that the Bible is infallible and that it is a rule of faith and conduct. But with the rise of liberalism, this vow was often reinterpreted to mean that the Bible was only infallible in matters of faith and morals. Thus the word *infallible* was watered down to allow errors of science and history, and this view is widely held among liberals today. To protect against this lower view of the Scriptures, conservative believers have found it necessary to use the additional adjective *inerrant*, which is to say that the Bible is without error.

To say the Bible is infallible ought to be enough. But in the current situation, we find it necessary to say also that the Bible is inerrant, if we mean that it is really true in all it says. The Bible is verbally inspired, it is infallible, and it is inerrant in the manuscripts as they were originally written. The statement of faith of the Evangelical Theological Society expresses it briefly but well: "The Bible alone, and the Bible in its entirety, is the Word of God written and is therefore inerrant in the autographs [original documents]."

Many think that this view of the Scriptures is too narrow. They say that in this twenty-first century, people cannot believe this. They say that the facts are against it, that the Bible's science is outmoded: We can no longer believe in a flat earth with heaven upstairs. They say that belief in a literal creation of a literal Adam or in the story of Jonah and other such tales must be denied. Indeed, they say, the Scriptures contradict themselves. They claim that there is a human element in Scripture that inerrancy does not allow for, and, therefore, by insisting on inerrancy, we will not reach modern people.

Some brief answers to these criticisms will be suggested here and will be developed in chapter 8. It may first be said that we should be slow to depart from an ancient doctrine—grounded as it has been on the teaching of Christ and His apostles—just to reach hypothetical "modern people." The prophets of old were commanded to preach the Word of God whether people would listen or not (see Isa. 6:9-10; Jer. 20:9; Ezek. 2:5-7).

Secondly, it is highly doubtful that the Bible pictures a flat earth with heaven upstairs. The claim is that it does if you "take it literally." But actually no one, not even the staunchest conservative, takes the Bible literally. The Bible is full of metaphors, parables, and poetry, which are to be interpreted as in any other piece of literature. How could anyone take "literally" such common expressions as "tickled to death," "a heart of gold," "ages since I saw you," etc. The objection depends on a crassly literal interpretation of various poetic passages and then says the Bible violates common knowledge. So would most poetry describing the moon, the trees, the mountains, and anything wonderful or beautiful.

Many forget that the standard astronomy of the New Testament world taught that the world is round. Eratosthenes had measured its circumference quite accurately in 250 B.C. It is curious that recent theologians who object to the idea that heaven is "up" speak of the "breaking in" of the kingdom of God. It is as strange to picture heaven this way, as outside a box, as it is to picture it as "up." But, as C. S. Lewis in his book *Miracles*[1] beautifully shows, all language about things that are not perceived by the senses must be metaphorical language. No other way can be found to describe the unseen.

So the Bible language does not mean to imply that the spiritual heaven is just upstairs (although Hebrew, like English, uses the same word for the heaven of stars and clouds and space where birds fly, which indeed is "up"). Similarly, "the ends of the earth" does not imply a falling-off place. The Hebrew word for "earth" is very often used for "land." The "ends of the earth" usually mean only distant places and the "four corners of the earth" refer only to wide areas in all directions (cf. Ezek. 7:2).

Thirdly, if people cannot believe in a literal creation, they must be able satisfactorily to ascribe to chance the marvelously intricate pattern of life, or, for that matter, the unique creature of intelligence, purpose, and moral consciousness that is known as man.

Finally, to object to the inerrancy of Scripture because of alleged contradictions neglects the years of study on these matters since the days of Justin who was martyred for the faith in A.D. 148 and who had written, "I am entirely convinced that no Scripture contradicts another" (*Dialogue with Trypho*, ch. 65).

It is obvious that the Bible contains some seeming difficulties and things that are hard to understand. Surely this is to be expected in a document from ancient times and from another culture. If culture shock is expected when traveling to foreign countries, how much more should surprising things be found in the Bible. But so many such difficulties have been solved by new discoveries about ancient practices and languages that an informed believer can attribute the few remaining problems to people's ignorance of the details of ancient life and history.

Factual problems continue to be answered to the satisfaction of a host of scholars today.

Conservative believers do not accept the idea that Scripture contains real contradictions. Like the early Church Fathers, they believe that such alleged contradictions are due to lack of knowledge or to minor errors of copying.

BIBLE INTERPRETATION (HERMENEUTICS)

The Protestant Reformation was a great "back-to-the-Bible" movement. The emphasis was on giving the Bible to the laity. Wycliffe had stood for the principle previously, but Luther, Tyndale, and others carried on the work of translating the Bible into the languages of the people. The corollary was that the Bible is a plain book that the common people can read and understand.

Certainly the history of succeeding years has supported this view. This does not mean, however, that everyone can fully understand every passage. Rather, any reader can learn of God and His way of salvation and can by faith accept it. But the judgments of God are unsearchable and "his ways past finding out" (Rom. 11:33). Even references to historical incidents and ancient daily practices are difficult for anyone who does not have the ancient and Eastern background information.

So the interpretation of the Bible in detail requires studying of ancient languages, culture, history, etc. But a new approach to hermeneutics says that the Bible is not relevant to us today. Advocates of this position say that ancient Jews lived too differently from us. They were not interested in exact figures, chronological relationships, or historical accuracy. Critics say the Bible was not wrong by its standards, but errs by modern scientific standards.

Several things should be mentioned in reply. First, the ancients were not so careless as some think. The pyramids, built five hundred years before Abraham, are oriented to the North Star to within five degrees! Hezekiah's engineers in about 732 B.C. dug a winding tunnel through eighteen hundred feet of rock in Jerusalem. They started from both ends and met in the middle, being only a foot or two off in their alignment.

Secondly, no one is always exact. Every carpenter knows that a 2"x4" stud used in house construction is only approximately 1½"x3½". Being approximate is not being wrong. Historical errors have been alleged in the Bible, but many times later archeological discoveries have shown that the Bible was right after all.

The argument has been overworked that says the Bible is not relevant for today because it is the product of the ancient world. Millions of people who have found comfort, meaning, and salvation through the Scriptures testify otherwise. And, although ancient culture differs much from the modern, the differences do not overshadow the similarities. People lived, loved, ate, were ill, fought, thought, sinned, and died as they do today. It is not true that the ancient mind was too different from modern man's. E. D. Hirsch calls this the fallacy of the inscrutable past.[2] He remarks that there is less difference between modern people and the ancients than there is between various modern people. The Bible is understandable, and it is relevant.

Others today who call themselves evangelical nonetheless hold that there are errors in the Bible. They claim, however, that these errors are only negligible and do not affect the spiritual message. They say that a strict inerrancy does not allow for the human element in the Bible.

But this view is based on a misconception. The historical concept of verbal inspiration and inerrancy assumes the view that God by His Spirit works powerfully on people, although His work is behind the scenes. The process of inspiration is not all of God and none of man—this would be dictation. Neither was it all of man and none of God—this would be humanism. Nor was it 50 percent of God and 50 percent of man—then errors of major magnitude would be inescapable.

But the real picture is that God used men in their total activity, and yet He worked upon them powerfully, being 100 percent in control. Hence, verbal inspiration is possible only because the Spirit of God is perfectly able to work like that. The result was that the Bible's authors wrote as no ordinary people wrote, but "as they were moved by the Holy Spirit" (2 Pet. 1:21). Like most spiritual truth, this view involves mystery. But it is a wonderful mystery, and it has given us an inerrant Bible.

THE IMPORTANCE OF THE INSPIRED SCRIPTURES

The view of verbal inspiration or inerrancy has been held by the leaders of the church since early days.[3] A view so widespread would surely be basic. One of the main emphases of the Reformation was *sola scriptura*: "The Bible alone." This emphasis was vital to that great spiritual renewal.

Due to liberal influences, the doctrine of inerrancy was largely lost in Germany in the nineteenth century and in many areas of America in the early twentieth century. A revival of full trust and belief in the Bible accompanied a real resurgence of evangelical strength and outreach in the later twentieth century. It is not difficult to see the connection.

Without a real and true word from heaven, people are lost in a sea of human opinion and moral weakness. The Ten Commandments have been taken out of public schools. Their authority has been denied in many of our older church bodies. The result is disastrous. But the warning was given long ago by the beloved disciple. "For I testify unto every man that heareth the words of the prophecy of this book, If any man shall add unto these things, God shall add unto him the plagues that are written in this book: And if any man shall take away from the words of the book of this prophecy, God shall take away his part out of the book of life, and out of the holy city, and from the things which are written in this book" (Rev. 22:18-19).

The Scriptures are God's Word to us. We should personally read them, study them, meditate upon them, and, most of all, practice them. And then we should join with others of like precious faith to see that the Scriptures are honored and taught to the ends of the earth.

VOCABULARY ENRICHMENT

general revelation, special revelation, infallible, inerrant, hermeneutics

DISCUSSION QUESTIONS

1. What does Romans 1:18-32 teach regarding whether people can actually find the true God by natural revelation?
2. If all men have consciences and so have a moral standard, why do they not live good and perfect lives?
3. What does Exodus 7:1 teach regarding a prophet being a spokesman for God?
4. Did the prophets of Baal, who were supported by Jezebel, really speak for their god, or did they just say what was popular (1 Kings 22:6)?
5. Compare Job 26:7 and 9:6. How can you explain the seeming contradiction here?

WHY CHRISTIANS BELIEVE THE BIBLE

Old Testament

The question, "Why do Christians believe the Bible?" can be answered in many ways. Some answers are more important than others. One group of answers is based largely on reasoning. Another set is based on faith. Both are basic and will be considered one by one. This chapter will present the answers related to the Old Testament. The next chapter will develop the reasons believers can have faith in the New Testament.

CHRIST BELIEVED IT

The easiest and clearest answer as to why Christians believe the Old Testament is that Christ believed it. We trust His teaching. The Lord Jesus Christ is our final authority in all matters. By miracles, wonders, and signs, He fully proved Himself to have come from God. He proved Himself to be the Son of God with power by the resurrection from the dead. Paul summarizes it in Romans 1:4: "And declared to be the Son of God with power, according to the spirit of holiness, by the resurrection from the dead." To doubt Christ's teachings is to doubt all that is precious and basic in the Christian faith. Jesus believed the Old Testament and taught its truth. That alone should be enough.

It is clear that Christ did believe and teach that the Old Testament is God's Word. Many specific verses give His teaching plainly, and many other passages in the Gospels indicate His general attitude toward the Old Testament.

Of primary importance is Christ's teaching to the two disciples on the road to Emmaus after His resurrection. Read Luke 24:13-31. In this account it is clear that the disciples had not fully accepted the testi-

mony of the women that Christ had risen. As He talked to the two disciples, He called them "fools, and slow of heart to believe all that the
prophets have spoken" (v. 25). Then He went through the Old
Testament, showing how it foretold these things. The Greek says, "He,
beginning, expounded to them from Moses and from all the prophets
in all the Scriptures the things concerning Himself" (v. 27). Notice how
Christ reasoned out of a book known both as "the Scriptures" and as
"Moses and all the prophets." The latter designation is a regular name for
the Old Testament in the Dead Sea Scrolls and in the New Testament. It
or "the law and the prophets" is used, with slight variations, several times
in the New Testament. Jesus was declaring that they should have believed
that book.

The same teaching is given forcefully in Luke 16:29-31. In this record
of the rich man and Lazarus, great emphasis is placed upon belief in
God's Word. The rich man was condemned to eternal torment from
which there was no escape or relief. Lazarus, "the beggar," was in the
place of eternal blessedness. The rich man pleaded with Abraham to send
Lazarus from the dead to warn his five living brothers. Christ quotes
Abraham's reply with obvious approval: "They have Moses and the
prophets"—the Old Testament. The tormented man still begged for a
special miraculous witness. Abraham replied, "If they hear not Moses
and the prophets, neither will they be persuaded, though one rose from
the dead" (v. 31).

Notice the force and application of this statement. The witness of
the Old Testament is more valuable than a resurrection testimony would
be. The Jewish leaders had made the Word of God of no effect through
their tradition. Notice also how this truth is borne out in subsequent
events. The Jews were not convinced by the resurrection of Lazarus of
Bethany or even by the resurrection of Christ Himself. The testimony
of the law and the prophets is final, just as Jesus has said.

Other passages bear the same witness. In John 10:33-39, Jesus quotes
from Psalm 82:6 calling it their "law" and argues that since "the scripture
cannot be broken," His own claims were justified. We are not now con-
sidering Christ's clear claim to deity. We are emphasizing the fact that
He grounded His claims upon Scripture—the unbreakable Scripture.
He had argued from the word *gods*. That one word was so certain that
He could make it the solid basis of His claim.

"For had ye believed Moses, ye would have believed me: for he wrote
of me. But if ye believe not his writings, how shall ye believe my words?"
(John 5:46-47). Here Christ spoke of Moses as the author of the first

five books of the Old Testament—the Pentateuch—and declares that we should believe these writings. Indeed Jesus ties up in the closest way belief in Moses' writings with belief in His own words. To doubt the Old Testament is to doubt Jesus. If we believe Jesus, we shall believe the Old Testament. These passages teach the importance of believing the Old Testament and the danger of denying it.

Further proof is recorded in Matthew 5:17-19 and Luke 16:16-17. Read these passages, which make it clear that Christ was referring to the Old Testament, "the law and the prophets." This title was used clearly enough to include just our thirty-nine Old Testament books. This book, "the law," is said to be letter perfect. The most stupendous claim is made for it: "It is easier for heaven and earth to disappear than for the least stroke of a pen to drop out of the Law" (Luke 16:17 NIV). Matthew is even more explicit: It is perfect "to the smallest letter . . . the least stroke of a pen." The King James Version says "the jot and tittle," which has become an English idiom. It is interesting to compare these passages with what Jesus said about His own words: "Heaven and earth shall pass away, but my words shall not pass away" (Matt. 24:35; Luke 21:33). Notice in passing that Jesus was not speaking of the preservation of His words, many of which have, of course, perished. He was speaking of their eternal truth and power—*the Word*.

Some people object to this appeal to Matthew 5:17, saying that Jesus proceeds to contradict the Scripture in the following verses. Here it is enough to say that Christ was not contradicting the Old Testament, but He was denying the traditional or scribal interpretations of it. For instance, in verse 43, "Ye have heard that it *hath been said* [not "it is written"], Thou shalt love thy neighbor, and hate thine enemy." Only the first part of this quotation (Lev. 19:18) is from the Old Testament. The last part is not. Jesus contradicted the last part—the Pharisaic addition. In similar verses, it can be shown that Jesus did not contradict the Old Testament itself. He exposed the scribal additions, mistranslations, and twistings. He honored the Old Testament itself as the sure Word of God.

Jesus' attitude toward the Old Testament is also shown in many general references. He quoted from it to banish Satan (Matt. 4:4, 7, 10). He began His ministry in Capernaum by reading Isaiah in the synagogue (Luke 4:16-19). To the assembled congregation He declared, "This day is this scripture fulfilled in your ears" (Luke 4:21). He told the Sadducees that they erred, "not knowing the scriptures" (Matt. 22:29). He appealed to the Scriptures to justify His own actions on the Sabbath (Matt. 12:5), His cleansing of the temple (Matt. 21:13), and His acceptance of the people's praise at His triumphal entry (Matt. 21:16). He declared that He must suffer in accordance with prophetic Scripture (Luke 18:31-34). He affirmed that Judas's action was foretold (Mark 14:21; John 13:18; 15:25). Jesus even refrained from calling on the angels for help that "the scriptures be fulfilled" (Matt. 26:54). His whole attitude was one of submission to the Scriptures. It is summed up in the remarkable verse: "But the scriptures must be fulfilled" (Mark 14:49). If Jesus thus accepted the Scripture, who are we to question or to deny it? Christians should believe and obey the Word of God.

Much more could be said. Jesus accepted the Old Testament's *acts* as well as its *teachings*, its *history* as well as its *doctrines*. He believed it all. He referred to Jonah and the huge fish (Matt. 12:40 NIV), the creation of Adam and Eve by God (Mark 10:6), Noah's ark (Matt. 24:38), and Lot's wife (Luke 17:32). In all the Gospels and in many passages, Jesus is presented consistently as fully believing the Old Testament. Today even most unbelieving scholars admit that Jesus did believe in the Old Testament. These unbelievers simply do not believe Jesus. But for the Christian, Christ's word is enough.

The Apostles Believed It

Further confirmation can be found in the attitude of the apostles who had learned from Christ. An outstanding example is in Paul's second letter to Timothy. This was Paul's last letter, and it is filled with serious admonitions. Paul wanted to leave Timothy with a solemn charge: "Preach the word" (2 Tim. 4:2). To emphasize this command, he reminds Timothy that "All scripture is given by inspiration of God, and is profitable for doctrine, for reproof, for correction, for instruction in righteousness" (2 Tim. 3:16).

Some have questioned the meaning of this verse, but there is no need to do so. The word *inspiration* does not mean "breathed in," but literally "God-breathed"—that is, spoken by God. There is no doubt as to what Scriptures are meant. Some would translate it, "Every Scripture inspired of God is also profitable" (RSV), as if only some Scriptures are in view. But the Scriptures referred to are made perfectly clear by verse 15. They were the Old Testament Scriptures that Timothy had learned at his Jewish mother's knee.

Peter's final epistle is equally explicit. He foresaw his coming death (2 Pet. 1:14) and was anxious to leave a worthy legacy. To keep his friends established in the faith, he recommends the prophetic Scriptures, which "came not in old time by the will of man: but holy men of God spake as they were moved by the Holy Ghost" (2 Pet. 1:21).

The other apostles quoted the Old Testament just as Jesus did. Whereas Jesus said that David wrote Psalm 110 by the Holy Spirit (Mark 12:36), Peter declared that David was a prophet and thus predicted Christ in Psalm 16 (Acts 2:30-31). Paul quoted Isaiah 6 and said that the Holy Spirit spoke this through Isaiah (Acts 28:25). Hebrews says the same thing: "God . . . spake . . . by the prophets" (Heb. 1:1).

The proof is complete and satisfying. Christ and the apostles whom He had taught accepted the Old Testament as the true and trustworthy Word of God.

Notice that Bible scholars do not here merely prove the Bible from the Bible. This is not circular reasoning. They first accept the New Testament as the solid historical account of Christ's life and teachings. The New Testament is plainly such an account. Then they investigate the teachings of Christ, examining how Christ proved Himself to be the truth and the source of eternal life. But not only this, Jesus taught that the thirty-nine Old Testament books, known as "the law and the prophets," were the revealed Word of God, true and without error even in detail.

This doctrine that Jesus Himself taught is usually called verbal inspiration. And on His authority we accept it. In former days Christians meant the same thing when they referred to Scripture as infallible or spoke of the plenary ("full" or "complete") inspiration of Scripture. This view of the Bible has been held by believing Christians of all ages. It is based upon the best of reasons, the witness of Christ Himself.

FACTS CONFIRM IT

There are many other factors that confirm the divine origin of the Old Testament. Any serious Bible student should be alert to and be able to evaluate these confirmations.

The Demonstration of Miracles

The miracles done by God's prophets as recorded in the Scriptures indicate that these men spoke from God.

The Confirmation of Prophecy

The Word of God contains hundreds of prophecies. Many of these have already been fulfilled—such as the dispersion of the Jews and the worldwide preaching of the Gospel. Others, such as Christ's second coming, are to be fulfilled at some future time.

This argument from prophecy will be pursued further in chapter 8. But at present note that the prophecies are evidences of the supernatural character of the Bible. They were intended to prove that God had spoken. That a prophecy had come to pass was one of the tests of a prophet of God as found in Deuteronomy 18:20-22. Micaiah prophesied in advance Ahab's death at Ramoth-Gilead and staked his claim to revelation in its fulfillment (1 Kings 22:28). Long-range prophecies, such as the prediction in Isaiah 44:26-28 that Cyrus would rebuild the temple at Jerusalem, are an example. And the predictions are often startlingly definite. Other books not dependent on the Bible do not give such prophecies. The Koran or sacred books of the East or the Christian Science book, *Science and Health, with Key to the Scriptures*, or the books of Greek philosophy—none of these attempt what the Bible does in hundreds of places scattered through all its major divisions. Skeptical minds seek explanations for this phenomenon. No satisfactory answer can be given apart from belief that Bible prophecy is a message from God, giving not merely impressions and feelings but definite information and revelations from above.

The Reality of Spiritual Truth

The Bible deals with heavenly and spiritual realities such as conversion, victory in Christ, the efficacy of prayer, and Christian fellowship. These and a great host of other divine realities bear testimony that the Bible is God's Word.

The Testimony of History

Another argument is that for centuries many people have been consistent in telling of the one true God, even in times when all other cultures of antiquity were sunk in polytheism and degradation. If we can judge by its fruit, the Bible is indeed from God.

FAITH AFFIRMS IT

At the beginning of this chapter, it was stated that some people believe the Bible because reason explains it. This is, in itself, not sufficient. The fact is that the best reasons will not convince an unbeliever. God-given faith is the convincing proof that the Bible is the very Word of God.

This does not mean that the above arguments or reasons are poor or inadequate. It simply means that the unsaved are blind to the Gospel. "Spiritual things . . . are spiritually discerned" (1 Cor. 2:13-14). Colorblind people cannot experience the difference between green and red. Blind individuals cannot see the sunlight.

Only as the Spirit of God operates on unregenerate hearts will unbelievers be able to fully believe the Bible. The unsaved may believe the Bible to be reliable history or sound advice. They may be impressed by its moral worth. But only the secret operation of the Holy Spirit can enable them to see the Bible for what it is—a revelation of God.

This truth is usually called the inner testimony of the Holy Spirit. We should be careful, however, that we understand this doctrine. Christians do not hear a voice saying, "This little black book is inspired." The Spirit does not give a witness or a light or revelation beyond the Bible. Rather He bears witness by and with the Word in our hearts. As Abraham Kuyper puts it, the Spirit witnesses to the "centrum," the basic facts of our salvation. The Bible gives us the way of salvation. The Spirit gives us eyes to see and accept and appreciate this salvation.

The Holy Spirit begets genuine heart faith through the preaching and teaching of the Gospel. People hear the facts of the gospel story— Jesus' life, death, and resurrection. They are convicted of sin by the Spirit and persuaded that Christ is the only Savior. "He that believeth on the Son of God hath the witness in himself. . . . And this is the record, that God hath given to us eternal life, and this life is in his Son. He that hath the Son hath life; and he that hath not the Son of God hath not life" (1 John 5:10-12). They have been converted and enabled to trust in Christ and to believe His teaching. These teachings include the fact that the Bible is the very Word of God. Such "believers" are children of God—Christians.

Christians "grow in grace" as they read and study the Bible. More and more they see the proofs of its divinity. They accept by *faith* and by *reason* the truth of its teachings about God, man, sin, and the Savior. The infallible proofs have been used by the Spirit to bring sinners to Christ and to open their eyes to accept "all that the prophets have spoken."

"These things have I written unto you that believe on the name of the Son of God; that ye may know that ye have eternal life, and that ye may believe on the name of the Son of God" (1 John 5:13).

VOCABULARY ENRICHMENT

Plenary inspiration, verbal inspiration.

DISCUSSION QUESTIONS

1. Using a concordance, locate all the New Testament occurrences of the term "Moses and the prophets" or the "law and the prophets."

2. What proof is there that Jesus taught the same thing about the Old Testament after His resurrection as before?

3. Memorize two or three texts showing Jesus' belief in the Scriptures.

4. What are your personal reasons for believing the Old Testament to be God's Word?

5. What did Jesus mean by His statement in Matthew 5:17?

6. Arrange a panel discussion, creating a probable situation in which a skeptic challenges a Christian with the question, "Why believe the Bible?"

WHY CHRISTIANS BELIEVE THE BIBLE

New Testament

Christians who believe the Old Testament usually have no difficulty believing the New Testament. This is natural. The New Testament gives the gospel story of Christ and the detailed history of the founding and spreading of the early church. Since the New Testament was written in more recent times than the Old Testament, there is abundant testimony by those who were contemporary with the authors or their immediate followers.

Anyone whose eyes have been opened by the Spirit to Old Testament truths will readily embrace the New. It is important, nevertheless, to be explicit about our beliefs in these matters and to study the evidences for the truth of the New Testament. Furthermore, a knowledge of the New Testament and its origin will add to the understanding of the origin of the Old.

In the case of the Old Testament, it is possible to quote Christ to the effect that the whole book is perfect and complete. This cannot be done with the New Testament, for it was written in its entirety after Christ ascended to heaven. We must therefore establish the principles that bear upon our belief in the New Testament from what Christ said beforehand and from what apostles have recorded of His teachings.

THE APOSTLES TESTIFY

The claims of the apostles in these matters are very explicit. Some skeptical people have assumed that the apostles had no idea that their writings would be received, collected together, and treasured as the Word of God. In the minds of such skeptics, Paul wrote letters much as we write letters today, and it was only in later times that they were venerated and then collected. This view denies any special gifts of the Spirit to the apostles. It denies that these writings were inspired by God. Such skepticism opposes the frequent claims of the apostles that they were intentionally writing to be believed and obeyed. Finally, it contradicts the plain facts of history that these books were received and treasured, not hundreds of years later, but as far back as present-day evidence goes—back to the days of the apostles themselves.

It is necessary to look closely at the claims of the apostles. These claims were made most prominently in connection with problems that arose when disobedient churches rebelled against their teachers. It is well known that this happened, especially in Corinth. What claims does Paul make for his authority, especially to the Corinthians?

Paul

Briefly, but emphatically, Paul claims to speak and to write the Word of God. First Corinthians was written to a divided, sinful, and rebellious church. Some of its members claimed spiritual gifts but did not demonstrate a spiritual attitude. In chapters 12 to 14, Paul gave them directions for the use of spiritual gifts. He closed with the rather sharp reminder: "What? came the word of God out from you? or came it unto you only? If any man think himself to be a prophet, or spiritual, let him acknowledge that the things that I write unto you are the commandments of the Lord" (1 Cor. 14:36-37). Paul here clearly claims God-given authority for his writings.

In 1 Thessalonians 2:13, the first epistle he ever wrote, Paul speaks similarly. He commends the Thessalonian Christians for faithfulness and declares that they had received his instruction as the Word of God, which it truly was, not the word of men. Shortly thereafter he wrote 2 Thessalonians because they misunderstood the Second Coming. In this epistle he speaks strongly: "And if any man obey not our word by this epistle, note that man, and have no company with him, that he may be ashamed" (2 Thess. 3:14). Paul gave his churches the Word of God and expected them to believe it and to obey it as such. First Corinthians 2 is an equally forceful section. In defense of his ministry, Paul declared that he spoke "in demonstration of the Spirit" (v. 4), speaking "the wisdom of God" (v. 7), as revealed to him "by his Spirit" (v. 10). He knew the things of God so revealed (v. 12), and he spoke them not in man's words, but in words "which the Holy Ghost teacheth" him (v. 13).

It is possible to miss this point because Paul uses the plural "we" in part of this section. This pronoun could refer to Paul and the other apostles, as in 1 Corinthians 4:9. More likely it is an editorial "we" that

Paul uses to speak modestly of himself. And in 2 Corinthians 10:8 he claims the same authority for "us" that he claims for himself personally ("my use of authority") in 2 Corinthians 13:10 (NASB).

Peter

Peter also believed that he wrote under the inspiration of God. In 2 Peter, his final letter, he emphasized the reliability of the Old Testament Scriptures. He also claimed that the gift of inspiration for the apostles was equal to that of the authors of the Old Testament: "Be mindful of the words which were spoken before by the holy prophets, and of the commandment of us the apostles of the Lord and Saviour" (2 Pet. 3:2). See also 2 Peter 1:16. These claims affirm that the Scriptures are to be received and believed.

Peter Approves Paul

Even more direct is Peter's reference to Paul: "Paul also wrote you with the wisdom that God gave him. He writes the same way in all his letters, speaking of them in these matters. . . . His letters contain some things that are hard to understand, which ignorant and unstable people distort, as they do the other Scriptures, to their own destruction" (2 Pet. 3:15-16 NIV). Here Peter asserts that Paul wrote Scriptures that, like the Old Testament, may be twisted, but only to the readers' peril. He specifically mentions certain "epistles" of Paul.

This passage in which Peter refers to the writings of Paul is remarkable as possibly the first instance of applying the term "Scripture" to other New Testament writings. Another place where this seems to have been done is 1 Timothy 5:18: "For the scripture saith, Thou shalt not muzzle the ox that treadeth out the corn. And, The labourer is worthy of his reward." This quotation consists of two statements. The first part is taken from Deuteronomy 25:4. The second quotation is identical (in the Greek) with Luke 10:7. It seems most natural to believe that Paul here quotes from the Old Testament and also from the third Gospel, calling both "Scripture."

A third passage of this nature is Jude 17-18. Here Jude recalls to mind "the words which were spoken before of the apostles of our Lord Jesus Christ." He quotes almost verbatim from 2 Peter 3:3. This quotation supports the apostolic authorship and early date of 2 Peter and shows the high regard for the apostolic company in those early days.

John

The concluding witness is the apostle John. In writing his gospel account, John clearly identifies himself as the beloved disciple who leaned on Jesus' breast at the Last Supper. He affirms that his writing and testimony are both true (John 21:20-24).

In the first epistle also, John presents a detailed claim that he was an eyewitness and that he was writing a message heard from God (1 John 1:1-5). He warns that false prophets are abroad and urges Christians to use discernment (4:1). Without hesitation he writes, "We are of God: he that knoweth God heareth us; he that is not of God heareth not us" (1 John 4:6). Meyer's commentary on this passage declares that it teaches that John and the other apostles spoke from God.

TESTIMONY OF REVELATION

Probably the most emphatic claims for New Testament Scripture are made by John in the book of Revelation. Many Christians apply these verses to the whole Bible, but their primary reference is to the book of Revelation. The principles, however, may be applied to the whole volume. The book, called "The Revelation of Jesus Christ Through John," has a salutation (1:4-5) like the writings of Paul. The book assures blessing for all who read, hear, and obey it (1:3). It pronounces a frightful curse on anyone who dares to "add unto" or "take away from the words of the book of this prophecy" (22:18-19). The reason is given by the revealing angel: "These sayings are faithful and true: and the Lord God of the holy prophets sent his angel to show unto his servants the things which must shortly be done. . . . blessed is he that keepeth the sayings of the prophecy of this book" (22:6-7). Later (v. 10) the Lord commands John to leave the sayings of the prophecy of this book unsealed. Note the contrast between this statement and Daniel 12:9 where the vision was to be "closed up and sealed till the time of the end." Revelation is actually put into the same class as the Old Testament. This was the apostolic position, and it must be our attitude toward the New Testament as a whole.

THE APOSTOLIC OFFICE

Why could the apostles speak thus of their own work? The answer is to be found in Christ's personal appointment of the Twelve and the fact that He personally promised their endowment with the Holy Spirit for their special work as teachers of the Word of God.

Consider the majesty of the office of apostle. Christ Himself selected the Twelve after His night of intercession (Luke 6:12-13). He later promised that they would "sit upon twelve thrones, judging the twelve tribes of Israel" (Matt. 19:28). Their names are inscribed on the twelve foundation stones of the New Jerusalem (Rev. 21:14). The church is "built upon the foundation of the apostles and prophets, Jesus Christ Himself being the chief corner stone" (Eph. 2:20). The apostles are first in the church (1 Cor. 12:28). The apostles, along with the Old Testament prophets, were ordained to this special privilege. The apostles were witnesses of Christ's resurrection (Acts 1:22). Christ promised that His Spirit would reveal to them God's Word.

In John's record of the Last Supper and subsequent events, many precious promises are given (John 13 to 17). In some cases, the apostles are distinguished from later Christians. In John 17:20, Jesus prayed, "Neither pray I for these alone, but for them also which shall believe on me through their word." John 14:26 and 16:13 are equally vivid. In John 14:26, the Holy Ghost was promised to the apostles. Though He comes to all Christians, this verse specifically promises that He would come to the apostles so that they might remember the words Jesus had spoken to them.

It is quite possible that the apostles had taken some notes of Jesus' messages. A system of shorthand was in use even in those days, and some of the apostles may have used it. Whether this was the case or not, the Holy Spirit was specifically promised to give them a remembrance of the gospel story. He was to guide them into all truth (John 16:13). Some Christians have uncritically held that this is a promise to the church at large. But the context clearly limits the promise of the Spirit's inspiring and revealing work to the apostles. He was promised to show "you things to come." This is not the Spirit's general illumination to all believers, but a specific promise to the Twelve.

What abundant proof of the New Testament's authenticity. Never cease to marvel at the way in which it was written. God who had spoken by the prophets sent His Son for our salvation. After Christ's ascension, the New Testament church was miraculously established at Pentecost. Its founders and leaders were chosen by Christ Himself. They were the apostles—with special gifts of inspiration and special apostolic signs to accompany their office. They claimed to speak and to write the Word of God the same as did the prophets of old. They called each other's writing "Scripture." They insisted that these writings should be read and obeyed. They spoke in Christ's name. They taught with His authority.

All branches of the church have historically held that the words of the apostles and of their assistants (such as Mark and Luke) are to be received as the very Word of God spoken. We are therefore fully justified in declaring that the New Testament, just like the Old Testament, was written by holy men of God moved by the Holy Spirit.

THE EARLY CHURCH FATHERS TESTIFY

The high regard for the apostles was shared by the early Church Fathers, who wrote immediately after the apostolic times.

Clement, Bishop of Rome

Clement, a bishop of the church in Rome, wrote a letter to the Corinthian Christians in A.D. 95. In it he referred to the "illustrious apostles," Peter and Paul. He said that the apostles preached the Gospel of Christ and were confirmed in the Word with full assurance of the Holy Spirit. He argued that they had perfect foreknowledge of church affairs. Finally, he said, "the blessed Apostle Paul" wrote to the Corinthians "under the inspiration of the Spirit" about the party strife that they showed toward the apostles (i.e., Peter and Paul) and "a man whom they have approved" (i.e., Apollos). Clearly, Clement revered the apostles and believed their writings.

Ignatius of Antioch

Ignatius lived in Clement's time. He was a bishop in the church at Antioch and was martyred either in A.D. 107 or 117. On his way to Rome for execution he wrote seven short epistles to different churches and individuals. Several times he contrasted himself with the apostles and lauded the apostles highly. For instance, in his letter to the Ephesians, he referred to "Paul the holy, the martyred, the deservedly most happy," who had written them an epistle. To the Romans he wrote, "I do not as Peter and Paul issue commandments unto you. They were apostles; I am but a condemned man."

Polycarp

Polycarp was also a famous martyr who gave his life for Christ at an advanced age. He died in about A.D. 155, having been a Christian (he said) for eighty-six years. In his youth he had known the apostle John. Ignatius wrote one of his letters to Polycarp. Polycarp's letter to the Philippians, written about A.D. 118, quoted from about half of the books of the New Testament. He referred to the apostles as parallel to the Old Testament prophets. He declared that he could not "come up to the wisdom of the blessed and glorified Paul," who had written them a letter. He referred to the martyrdom of Ignatius but reserved the classification of apostle for Paul and men like him.

Other Church Fathers

Other authors, such as Papias, Ireneaus, and Tertullian, provide more specific references to such things, so that we have much testimony from the next generation of men.

Chronology of Some Church Fathers and Writings

A.D.

95	Clement of Rome
117	Ignatius
117	Polycarp's Letter
130	Epistle of Barnabas
145	Papias
145	Justin Martyr, Barnabas, Hermas,
160	Epistles of Hermas
160	*Didache* (di-da-kay) or Teaching of the Twelve Apostles
170	Irenaeus, Muratorian Fragment
200	Tertullian, Clement of Alexandria

VOCABULARY ENRICHMENT

Apostle, Clement, early Church Fathers, Ignatius, Polycarp, Revelation.

DISCUSSION QUESTIONS

1. Compare the list of apostles in Matthew 10:2-4; Luke 6:14-16; and Acts 1:13, 26.
2. In 1 Corinthians 2:13 and 1 Thessalonians 2:13, how does Paul claim that his writings are true? What did he say regarding the inspiration of his public verbal teaching?
3. In what two passages do New Testament books call other New Testament books Scripture?
4. How did Paul fit the test that an apostle must be a witness of the resurrection of Jesus (1 Cor. 15:8-9)?
5. Can anyone properly be called an apostle today? What reasons can you give in support of your answer (Acts 1:22)?
6. What curses are given in Revelation for those who alter Scripture? What is promised for those who read it and keep it?
7. What reasons are there for personally accepting the New Testament as equally inspired with the Old Testament?
8. Examine the chronology chart above.

WHO WROTE THE
OLD TESTAMENT?

God could have communicated His will and His work to us in dozens of ways. He chose the writing of the Bible to reveal His wisdom and truth. Before Moses' day, God evidently spoke directly to Adam, Cain, Enoch, Noah, Abraham, and others. These men communicated God's Word to others by word of mouth. Apparently it was not written down. Indeed, there were ages during which writing had not yet been invented. Eventually, however, God commissioned certain men to write down the message He had given to them.

A study of inspiration shows that God wrote the sacred volume by His Spirit. The Bible is also a divine library with many human authors. It is our purpose to study these human authors, but we must always remember that the Bible is a single volume, one book, written by one Author, the Holy Spirit. This book has one great theme, redemption, and one great historical thread, God's saving dealings with fallen mankind.

MOSES

The first author of the Scripture was Moses, with whom God spoke "mouth to mouth, even apparently, and not in dark speeches" (Num. 12:8). Moses wrote the first five books called the Pentateuch or Law of Moses. The Jewish name is Torah (Law). He also wrote Psalm 90.

Never depreciate or minimize the work of the Holy Spirit when speaking of Moses' genius, for the Lord gave him his genius and his training. When God has a work to be done, He chooses the right man to do it. Moses was that man. Moses stood at the threshold of a new day. God had previously dealt with individuals and families. Now, in accordance with His promise to Abraham, He would weld Israel into a nation. Through God's providence, Moses, a slave by birth, "was learned in all the wisdom of the Egyptians" (Acts 7:22). He had learned of Israel's

God at his mother's knee, for she cared for her own son as Pharaoh's daughter's hired nurse.

At Pharaoh's court Moses studied reading, writing, and Egyptian culture. He learned the Egyptian and Akkadian (Babylonian) languages, in addition to his native Hebrew. He probably studied the Babylonian classics, civil administration, and military science. All this training and inborn ability was used in later years when God made him the leader of the nation, the judge of Israel, the captain of the army, the architect of the tabernacle, the people's poet, and the divine prophet and lawgiver. What a chosen vessel was Moses! What a man of God!

Moses was probably born about 1520 B.C., during one of the greatest periods of Egypt's history. His writings are known and loved around the world. He stands at the head of a long line of Old Testament prophets who revealed God's will to Israel for more than 1,000 years.

THE PROPHETIC LINE

God provided tests by which prophets were to be judged (Deut. 13 and 18). False prophets were those who disagreed with the true revelation already given and whose predictions did not come true. Exodus 4:1-5 shows that miracles also were given as a certification of the prophet's word. By these standards, Israel knew who God's true prophets were and which prophets were false. All the true prophets typified the great Prophet to come, Jesus Christ.

We do not know the names of all the prophets, but we do know many of them. Samuel wrote at least one book about the kingdom when Saul was anointed king (1 Sam. 10:25). He wrote a history of David's reign (1 Chron. 29:29) and delivered many prophecies. David, sweet singer and great king, was also a prophet (Acts 2:30). He wrote about half of the book of Psalms. From David to Malachi there were dozens of prophets. In this group were Elijah and Elisha, about 850 B.C.; Isaiah, Hosea, Joel, about 725 B.C.; Jeremiah, Nahum, Habakkuk, and Zephaniah about 600 B.C.; Ezekiel, Daniel, and others of captivity and post-captivity days to about 400 B.C.

There was also a succession of lesser-known prophets who recorded the history of the same period. These prophets are mentioned in a chain of references in Chronicles. For David's era, 1 Chronicles 29:29 mentions Samuel, Nathan, and Gad. For Solomon, 2 Chronicles 9:29 names Ahijah and Iddo. In 2 Chronicles 12:15, Shemaiah is also listed for the history of Rehoboam. Others were Jehu, the son of Hanani, who wrote of Jehoshaphat (2 Chron. 20:34), and Isaiah, who wrote of

Uzziah and Hezekiah (2 Chron. 26:22 and 32:32). Many other prophets are mentioned.

Most Old Testament books were written by prophets whose names we know. The others are included in the "more sure word of prophecy" (2 Pet. 1:19) and the books of the "prophets which are read every sabbath" (Acts 13:27). An examination of the Old Testament will reveal much detail about their writing.

Between the Pentateuch and David's time, Israel's history is given in Joshua, Judges, Ruth, and possibly Job. It is not specifically known who wrote Joshua, but Joshua himself probably wrote it or at least part of it. He was filled with the Spirit (Deut. 34:9), the people feared him as they had Moses (Josh. 4:14), and he wrote the words of the covenant in the Book of the Law of God (Josh. 24:26). He used the prophets' formula: "Thus saith the Lord" (Josh. 24:2). One apocryphal book, written in the time between the Testaments, calls Joshua the "successor of Moses in prophecies" (Ecclesiasticus 46:1).

Judges and Ruth present the period from Joshua to Samson. Judges portrays the sinfulness of those days (Judg. 17—21). Ruth is a beautiful picture of the godly who maintained the faith through dark days. Ruth was the great-grandmother of David. Judges-Ruth were united in one book in the old Hebrew enumeration and were probably written at the close of this period.

Job presents special considerations. Conservative scholars believe that this book is quite old, possibly written before Moses. It is argued that Job does not mention tabernacle worship. Instead, Job sacrificed at his sons' houses, much as Abraham offered private sacrifices. Other scholars have placed Job quite late. Their arguments are based on its style and its theology. These are the same arguments often given for the lateness of other books that the Bible specifically calls early. We cannot accept the arguments for its extreme lateness.

David, about 1000 B.C., is the chief author of the Psalms. Heman, Asaph, and other authors are referred to as prophets of God (1 Chron. 25:5; 2 Chron. 29:30). Eighteen psalms have no titles, but the Greek Septuagint translation assigns some to Haggai, Zechariah, and others.

Solomon wrote Ecclesiastes, the Song of Songs (Song of Solomon), and most of the Proverbs. It is now possible to place Solomon's reign at about 960-920 B.C. Archeological discoveries have shown Solomon's reign to be the time of Israel's greatest material success. Under his leadership, the worship of God at the new temple was established and furthered. He was a suitable author for the books that the Jews call Wisdom

Literature. The burden of Proverbs is that "the fear of the LORD is the beginning of wisdom" (Prov. 9:10). It is not merely a book of worldly-wise sayings. It contrasts good and evil and shows the necessity of trust in the Lord (Prov. 22:19). In Proverbs, the "wise" man is the godly man, and the "fool" is the sinner. The final chapters, called "prophecy" by men unknown to us (Prov. 30:1; 31:1), may have been added later.

Ecclesiastes, a book of philosophy, raises the question, "What is the chief end of man?" Various unsatisfactory answers are given and examined. The final answer of the "Preacher, the son of David, king in Jerusalem" is "Fear God, and keep his commandments" (Eccles. 12:13).

Solomon's Song of Songs is a poem of true love, typifying God's love for His people. Its conclusion may well be translated, "love is strong as death; jealousy is cruel as the grave. . . . Many waters cannot quench love" (Song of Sol. 8:6-7).

Solomon's writings, composed in his early years, were included in the Scriptures said to be given by God through "his prophets" (Rom. 1:2). Proverbs is quoted in the Dead Sea Scrolls of the second century B.C. with the phrase reserved for Scripture: "It is written."

Three great cycles of prophetic activity complete the Old Testament. In the 700s, God raised up great prophets to warn and comfort Israel during the Assyrian menace. These included Isaiah, the "evangelical prophet," and several of the Minor Prophets. Joel, Amos, and Jonah may have been the earliest of these. Isaiah, Hosea, and Micah soon followed. Obadiah is not dated but may be placed in this period because of its traditional position between Amos and Jonah. Of these, Hosea and Amos prophesied to the Northern Kingdom, which was carried off after several invasions to Assyria in 721 B.C.

During the century beginning about 625 B.C., Jeremiah ministered to the dying kingdom of Judah. This period also witnessed three Minor Prophets—Nahum, Habakkuk, and Zephaniah—all of whom predicted the downfall of Nineveh, the Assyrian capital. It fell in about 612 B.C. Shortly thereafter Nebuchadnezzar brought Babylon to the peak of its power. In expanding his conquests to the west, he broke the power of Egypt and finally demolished Judah in a series of attacks in 604, 597, and 586 B.C. The pitifully small group of captives taken to Babylon marked the end of real Jewish independence until A.D. 1948.

During the exile, Ezekiel and Daniel prophesied to the remnant in Babylon. These men did much to keep alive the true faith in those dark days. Their prophecies predicting the Messiah as Israel's hope brought into focus the great Messianic revelations of David, Isaiah, Micah, and others.

After the exile, the Jews returned to Palestine in three stages. In 538 B.C., Cyrus let the Jews return under Zerubbabel. At this time Haggai and Zechariah prophesied to the people in Jerusalem and encouraged them to build the second temple in 516 B.C. About this same time, Esther was written in Mesopotamia to show God's providential care over the captives who had remained behind, as well as to emphasize the dangers the Jews were exposed to while living under the pagan kings of Persia. Haman's massacre probably made many more Jews ready for the later stages of the return.

These later returns took place in 456 and 444 B.C. Ezra and then Nehemiah returned to rebuild the city and the wall. The first chapters of Ezra tell about the earlier return of Zerubbabel in 538 B.C. The rest of Ezra and all of Nehemiah trace the history to about 400 B.C. Malachi, last of the Minor Prophets, completed the Old Testament in about 400 B.C., after which the voice of prophecy was stilled. According to Jewish tradition and history, there was no prophet until John the Baptist announced the coming of a new age.

Thus the Old Testament was written from 1400 B.C. to 400 B.C. by more than twenty known authors and some unknown writers. The English Old Testament is conveniently divided into five groups of books. This division is a modification of the Latin Bible from the Greek Septuagint.

> 5 — The Law
> 12 — History
> 5 — Poetry
> 5 — Major Prophets
> 12 — Minor Prophets
> 39

Dates of Old Testament Books

B.C.

1400	Genesis, Exodus, Leviticus, Numbers, Deuteronomy
1400	Job (?)
1350	Joshua
1050	Judges-Ruth
1000	Psalms (the majority)
1000-575	1, 2 Samuel; 1, 2 Kings
950	Proverbs, Ecclesiastes, Song of Solomon
750-700	Isaiah, Hosea, Joel (?), Amos, Obadiah (?), Jonah, Micah
625-575	Jeremiah, Nahum, Habakkuk, Zephaniah
600-539	Ezekiel, Daniel
539-515	Haggai, Zechariah
475	Esther
456-400	1, 2 Chronicles, Ezra, Nehemiah, Malachi

The Hebrew Old Testament is now arranged in three divisions—the Law, Prophets, and Writings. There are five books of the Law, four books of earlier Prophets, four books of later Prophets (the twelve Minor Prophets count as one book), and eleven books of Writings. The total of twenty-four books includes, in various combinations, all of our thirty-nine books and no others.

Our present threefold division is perhaps due to liturgical usage and can be traced back to about A.D. 200. Before that a threefold division was used (along with the twofold "law and prophets"), but the books in each division were different. Two of the smaller books had been combined with others. Josephus (see below) put five books in the Law, thirteen in the Prophets, and four in a third division.

The Dead Sea Scrolls refer to the whole volume as "the work of Moses and the Prophets." Jesus referred to this book after His resurrection when He challenged His apostles to believe "all that the prophets have spoken" (Luke 24:25).

THE APOCRYPHA

Seven other complete books and a few additions are included in Roman Catholic Bibles. These additions are called the Apocrypha. A study of their origin will show why Protestants do not include them.

The Names of the Apocryphal Books

The Apocryphal books were evidently written during the period between the Old and New Testaments. Only one is dated. Two books, Judith and Tobit, tell of the Assyrian and Babylonian invasions. Two more, 1 and 2 Maccabees, record the Jewish War of Independence at about 165 B.C. Two more are books of wisdom—Ecclesiasticus and Wisdom of Solomon. One is an addendum to Jeremiah. There are also short additions to Esther and Daniel.

Several other books written during this period are not accepted by either Romanists or Protestants. These give the history and thought of the intertestamental period. They are such books as Enoch, Jubilees, and Testament of the Twelve Patriarchs. Fragments of these have been found among the Dead Sea Scrolls. These books were not received or quoted as Scripture. They are of some value but have never been in the canon.

Josephus, the Jewish Historian

How can we be sure these books should not be included in the Old Testament canon? It is certain they were not in the Scripture recognized and used by Christ and the apostles. The Jewish historian Josephus, who wrote in about A.D. 90, lived during the fall of Jerusalem in A.D. 70. His autobiography tells how the Emperor Titus gave him the sacred scrolls from the temple at Jerusalem when it was pillaged. He was qualified to know the canon of Jesus' day. In a significant writing, he says:

> *We have not an innumerable multitude of books among us disagreeing and contradicting one another, but only twenty-two books which contain the records of all the past times, which are justly believed to be divine. And of them, five belong to Moses, which contain his laws, and the traditions of the origin of mankind till his death. This interval of time was little short of three thousand years. But as to the time from the death of Moses till the reign of Artaxerxes, king of Persia, who reigned after Xerxes, the prophets, who were after Moses, wrote down what was done in their times in thirteen books. The remaining four books contain hymns to God and precepts for the conduct of human life. It is true our history hath been written since Artaxerxes very particularly, but hath not been esteemed of a like authority with the former by our forefathers, because there hath not been an exact succession of prophets since that time, and how firmly we have given credit to these books of our nation, is evident by what we do; for during so many ages as have already passed, no one hath been so bold as either to add anything to them, to take anything from them, or to make any change in them; but it has become natural to all Jews, immediately and from their very birth, to esteem these books to contain divine doctrines, and to persist in them, and, if occasion be, willingly to die for them.*

This quotation teaches several things. First, the Jews believed in verbal inspiration. Second, they received the canonical books because these were written by prophets. Third, it was known that the Apocryphal books and others were not written by prophets. Fourth, the canon included all of our thirty-nine books and no others. Fifth, but very important, Josephus gives the first and only listing until about A.D. 170 of the Old Testament books. They were listed in three divisions, which are not the same as the three divisions common among the later Jews and found in modern Hebrew Bibles. Josephus placed the Pentateuch first, then all the books of Prophecy and History, then four books of Poetry and instruction (probably Psalms, Proverbs, Song of Songs, and Ecclesiastes). Sixth, he gave great prominence to prophetic authorship.

The New Testament quotes from almost all thirty-nine canonical books but not once from the Apocrypha. Jesus referred to the Old Testament once as "the law of Moses," "the prophets," and "the psalms"

(Luke 24:44). The New Testament often cites the Old Testament in two divisions—the Law and the Prophets or Moses and all the Prophets (Matt. 5:17; Luke 16:29; 24:27). It never cites the Apocrypha.

Dead Sea Scrolls

The Dead Sea Scrolls supply further confirmation. They indicate that the Scriptures are the word of Moses and the prophets. They quote many Old Testament books as Scripture but none of the Apocrypha.

Septuagint

The situation is a closed case except for one problem. Present-day copies of the Septuagint contain the Apocrypha. Since the New Testament frequently quotes from the Septuagint Old Testament, many scholars argue that the New Testament sanctions the Apocrypha. It is important, however, to know that our Septuagint copies come from a late time—about A.D. 325. There is no evidence that the early Septuagint contained the Apocrypha. Indeed there is evidence against it.

Early Church Fathers

Most of the early Church Fathers who touch on this subject excluded the Apocrypha. Melito, a bishop of Sardis in A.D. 170, listed the Old Testament books paralleling our listing, and he excluded the Apocrypha. The learned Origen of Egypt in A.D. 250 also excluded the Apocrypha. Jerome, who translated the Apocryphal books into Latin, explicitly said they were non-canonical. Only two ancient councils, and those not widely authoritative, approved the Apocrypha. A later one was the Roman Catholic Council of Trent in A.D. 1545, when the Romanists, in opposition to the Protestants, insisted that the Apocrypha was inspired. There is hardly a shakier point in Roman Catholic theology.

We believe that the thirty-nine canonical books of the Old Testament are the inspired Word of God. The Apocryphal books are not. The thirty-nine were approved by Jesus and the apostles. The others were not. Most of these thirty-nine were clearly written by prophets. If Samuel and Kings are the work of the succession of prophets mentioned in Chronicles (1 Chron. 29:29; 2 Chron. 9:29; 12:15; 20:34; 26:22; 32:32), and if Solomon received visions as a prophet from God, then at least thirty of the Old Testament books were written by prophets. The other nine may have been written by prophets. They are included with the thirty as the work of prophets by the New Testament, the Dead Sea Scroll authors, and Josephus. The Apocrypha and other books have no such claim to be a revelation from God. We may read the Apocrypha for information and insights into the history and culture of the intertestamental period and what life was like at the time of Christ, but we reserve our faith and confidence for the books approved by Christ. "They have Moses and the prophets; let them hear them" (Luke 16:29).

VOCABULARY ENRICHMENT

Apocrypha, Pentateuch, Septuagint, Torah

DISCUSSION QUESTIONS

1. Memorize the books of the Old Testament. Check your spelling and pronunciation of these names.
2. Could a prophet also be a king (Acts 2:30)? A priest (Ezek. 1:3)?
3. What prophet was predicted as yet to come when the Old Testament closed (Mal. 4:5; Matt. 17:12-13; Luke 1:17)?
4. Compare our popular division of the Old Testament into five parts with the Hebrew three-part division.
5. Try to obtain a copy of the works of Josephus and read what he says about the Old Testament books in *Against Apion*, book 1, chapter 8.
6. How do the Hebrew Scriptures of twenty-two books include all thirty-nine books of our Old Testament canon?
7. What is meant by apocryphal books?
8. Why are apocryphal books not included in the canonical list?
9. Study the chart "Dates of Old Testament Books" in this chapter. Arrange the books in their correct time periods under the following headings: Beginnings to Wilderness Wanderings, In the Promised Land, In Exile, The Exiles Return.

5

WHO WROTE THE NEW TESTAMENT?

Peter refers to the whole Bible when he admonishes us to "be mindful of the words which were spoken before by the holy prophets, and of the commandment of us the apostles of the Lord and Saviour" (2 Pet. 3:2).

Any study of the writing of the New Testament must emphasize the importance of the apostolic office. It should consider the details of the various books, their dates, and their authorship. Also such study would be incomplete without a brief review of the Christian literature written immediately after the days of the apostles. These writings provide external evidence of the various books' authorship and their acceptance and recognition as parts of the Bible.

THE CHURCH FATHERS

The previous chapters have already discussed some of the early Church Fathers, or "Apostolic Fathers," as they are often called. These include Clement of Rome, Ignatius of Antioch, and Polycarp. These men were discussed in relationship to New Testament authority. They are also important in establishing New Testament authorship. We shall see below how their writings support the genuineness of Paul's writings and the writings of other apostles in the New Testament.

Papias

An important link is Papias, who lived about A.D. 140. He tells how he had diligently searched out the traditions of the apostles from those who had personally heard them. In this context he mentioned seven of the twelve apostles. It is known that he wrote a five-volume book on the Gospels. This book has, however, been lost, but some quotations from it tell how the Gospels were written. These excerpts are preserved in Eusebius's *Church History*, written about A.D. 300.

Justin

Slightly later than Papias is Justin, about A.D. 145. Before being martyred for his faith, he wrote several books, seven of which are left. His witness to the Gospels is examined later in this chapter.

General Writings of the Fathers

Several other writings of about this time are known, but their authorship is uncertain. These include *The Epistle of Barnabas, Teaching of the Twelve Apostles* (called *Didache*), and the allegory called *The Shepherd of Hermas*. Numerous other early books have been lost. The so-called *Gospel of Truth*, written about A.D. 140 and long lost, has recently been rediscovered. It is not itself valuable, but is a good witness to the early use of many of our New Testament books.

The above list covers the literature to about A.D. 145—fifty years after the last apostle's death. The writing that has been preserved is interesting and valuable. It breathes the air of real Christian devotion.

After A.D. 170, the literature that remains is much more extensive. A work by Irenaeus in A.D. 170 covers more than 250 large pages of English text. His writing is especially important because he was a pupil of Polycarp and therefore linked closely with the apostle John.

This same period provides an invaluable catalog of New Testament books called the Muratorian Fragment, part of which has been destroyed.

Dating about A.D. 200 are extensive writings by Tertullian, who lived in North Africa across from Spain. Clement of Alexandria, Egypt, also wrote at this time (see chart on p. 29).

These early witnesses tell much about the formation of the New Testament. But it is the student's task to combine the ancient, external, Christian witness with the internal witness that the New Testament bears to its own authorship and formation. Therefore, we turn to the New Testament writings themselves and combine with their internal evidence the testimony of the Fathers introduced above.

PAUL'S WRITINGS

The writings of Paul are of primary importance because many of his epistles tell us when they were written. Thirteen epistles, from Romans to Philemon, begin with statements that include Paul's name. Today even critical students admit that most of these letters were written by Paul. There is no objective evidence against the Pauline authorship of any of them.

In Galatians Paul tells something about his life. He saw Peter in

Jerusalem three years after his conversion (Gal. 1:18). Over fourteen years later, he went to Jerusalem again with Barnabas and Titus (Gal. 2:1).

The information and other data in Corinthians and in Acts indicate that Paul was converted in the early thirties and was with Peter in Jerusalem in about A.D. 37 or 38. Paul's witness to the events of Christ's life, therefore, goes right back to the earliest apostolic community in Jerusalem. This is extremely important since it validates Paul's detailed witness to Jesus' resurrection (1 Cor. 15:1-20). Reading the record makes it possible for the reader, as it were, to stand by the empty tomb in Jerusalem within about five years of Christ's resurrection.

Acts teaches the facts of Paul's three missionary journeys and his imprisonment in Palestine for two years and then in Rome for two years. Various hints make it clear that he wrote no epistles on the first journey in southern Asia Minor. During his second journey, which took him through Greece, he stayed at Corinth almost two years and wrote two epistles, 1 and 2 Thessalonians. These should be studied in the light of Acts 18. They are brief epistles dispatched after Paul had received good news of the infant church at Thessalonica. They stress salvation through the divine Christ (1 Thess. 1:9-10) and clearly demonstrate the authority of the apostle (1 Thess. 2:13; 2 Thess. 3:14-17).

Next Paul wrote the so-called major epistles. Galatians was probably written at the start of his third journey. During this time, he stayed at Ephesus about three years and wrote three epistles—Romans, 1 and 2 Corinthians (read Acts 19). Romans and Galatians should be studied together because of similarity in structure, subject matter, and phraseology.

At the end of the third missionary journey, Paul was taken prisoner in Jerusalem. An interesting phenomenon occurs in the book of Acts. In some passages, such as Acts 16:10, the author says "we" went on certain journeys. In others (Acts 20:13-14), the "we" refers to one group of the missionary party traveling on while Paul went a different way by himself. The logical conclusion is that Acts was written by someone who usually traveled with Paul. These "we" sections show that the author went with Paul on his last trip to Jerusalem. This man was undoubtedly free in Palestine for two years while Paul was in jail. Later he accompanied Paul on the shipwreck journey to Rome (Acts 27:2) and was free in Rome for two years while Paul was in bonds there. The Muratorian Fragment, Irenaeus, and other early witnesses name this helper as Luke.

While Paul was in bonds at Rome, he wrote the four important Prison

Epistles—Ephesians, Philippians, Colossians, and Philemon. Colossians and Ephesians have much in common and should be studied together.

Philippians 1:12-25 indicates that Paul was expecting trial and release. This evidently happened, for as he traveled, he left his coat and books at Troas (2 Tim. 4:13). During this time, he wrote the Pastoral Epistles—Titus and 1 and 2 Timothy. First Timothy and Titus are quite similar and help to explain each other. Each gives details about the organization of churches and the qualifications of church officers.

Table of Paul's Writings

Journeys	Writings
First Missionary Journey (in Asia Minor only)	No epistles
Second Missionary Journey (through Asia Minor and Greece; two years at Corinth)	1 Thessalonians 2 Thessalonians
Third Missionary Journey (same territory as second; three years at Ephesus)	Romans 1 Corinthians 2 Corinthians Galatians (or earlier)
Imprisonment in Palestine for two years	No epistles Luke's Gospel (see p. 45)
First Imprisonment in Rome for two years	Prison Epistles Ephesians Philippians Colossians Philemon Acts (see p. 45)
Period of Liberty Travel to Troas and Spain (?)	1 Timothy Titus Hebrews (?)
Second Imprisonment in Rome and martyrdom	2 Timothy

Second Timothy was Paul's last epistle. He was arrested again and doubtless executed (2 Tim. 4:7-8). Clement of Rome in A.D. 95 said that Paul preached in the "extreme limit of the West," fulfilling his desire to visit Spain (Rom. 15:24) after his first Roman imprisonment.

The Pauline Epistles are all used by writers before A.D. 120—thirty years after the death of the last apostle. Some of them were referred to by name.

For instance, Clement, writing in A.D. 95 to the Corinthians, refers expressly to Paul's having written to them. Ignatius in A.D. 117, writing to the Ephesians, refers either to Paul's epistles to them or to his epistles in general. Polycarp, writing to the Philippians in about A.D. 118, refers to Paul's epistle to them and quotes from six of Paul's other epistles.

LUKE'S GOSPEL

Luke was intimately associated with Paul. Acts 1:1 explains that this was the author's second writing to Theophilus. Obviously, from Luke 1:1-3, we see that the Gospel of Luke was Luke's first one. The New Testament does not specifically state that Luke was the author of Luke's Gospel or the Acts of the Apostles, but it is clear from the "we" sections that some companion of Paul wrote them. Also the history of the book of Acts has been supported even in small detail by the research of William Ramsey[1] and others. The name and title of Gallio (Acts 18:12), the titles of Sergius Paulus (Acts 13:7) and other officials, and also other historical details are so precise that the most natural conclusion is that it was written by a man contemporary with the events. Luke's Gospel, of course, preceded Acts (Acts 1:1).

Luke's Gospel and Acts were used by both Ignatius and Polycarp. Justin Martyr quoted from the three Synoptic Gospels and probably from John, calling them together "The Memoirs of the Apostles." He gives an interesting description of a Sunday service in which "the Memoirs of the Apostles or the Writings of the Prophets" were read, followed by a sermon. He spoke of the Gospels as the "memoirs which I say were drawn up by His apostles and those who followed them." In this quotation, he shows that Luke and Mark were not directly written by apostles, although elsewhere he calls these books the work of apostles.

In A.D. 170 the Muratorian Fragment and Irenaeus explain that Luke wrote the Gospel, but wrote in some sort of association with Paul. Tertullian, about A.D. 200, ascribed it to Luke, writing under Paul's supervision. He intimates that it can be called Pauline. Origination by the apostle seems to fit all the facts. In 1 Timothy 5:18, Paul quotes briefly from Deuteronomy and from Luke 10:7 in connection with salaries for ministers. In 1 Corinthians 9:7-18, he had argued that same subject quoting extensively from the Old Testament, but not from Luke. The "Table of Paul's Writings" clearly demonstrates that between the writing of 1 Corinthians and 1 Timothy, Paul was imprisoned in Palestine, while Luke was free. These reasons and other evidence lead to the belief that Luke gathered his material and wrote the third Gospel at that time. The book of Acts would have been written shortly afterward, probably during Paul's Roman imprisonment. Both books could have been written by Luke as Paul's understudy.

THE HEBREW EPISTLE

Was the Epistle to the Hebrews written by Paul? If so, when and how? Devout scholars do not agree on the answers to these questions. Some believe that it was written somewhat like Luke and Acts—by one of Paul's helpers under his supervision.

The Epistle to the Hebrews was known and used as early as Clement of Rome in A.D. 95. It was first accepted widely, then questioned in the West, and finally accepted by the entire church. There is little question about its canonicity. The main problem has been its obscure authorship. Wherever its Pauline authorship has been believed, the Epistle has been accepted without question. In Egypt the tradition of Pauline authorship dates back to Clement of Alexandria (A.D. 200), and before him to Pantaenus. Like Polycarp, Pantaenus lived to a great age and connected the Alexandrian church with the early days.

All the facts seem to harmonize when the Epistle is considered Pauline, but that it probably was written down or even translated by Luke or Barnabas or someone similar. It is fairly well established that Paul used stenographers, as Romans 16:22 shows. Origen (d. A.D. 250) has often been quoted as saying, "Who wrote the epistle, in truth, only God knows."[2] But in the context, Origen is talking about the penman and argues that Paul is behind the epistle. In his work *De Principiis*, Origen refers to Hebrews over half a dozen times as by Paul,[3] and in his book *Ad Africanus* he claims specifically that Paul can be proved to be the author.[4] The Chester Beatty Papyrus of the Pauline Epistles comes from about A.D. 200, and it includes Hebrews, placing it between Romans and Corinthians. In any event, Hebrews was probably written during Paul's later life.

MATTHEW'S GOSPEL

The Gospel of Matthew is the one to which we have earliest outside reference. It is used by Clement, Ignatius, Polycarp, and others. Barnabas quoted it with the phrase "it is written." It was never questioned in antiquity. Papias suggests that Matthew wrote in Aramaic, and the Gospel was translated later. If this is true, the Aramaic original has perished. Matthew himself may have published the book in Aramaic and Greek. This was frequently done because both languages were used in Palestine.

This much is obvious: Matthew's Gospel was written with special attention to the Jews who formed the bulk of the earliest Christian church.

MARK'S GOSPEL

Mark wrote the second Gospel, according to Papias, as Peter's helper or interpreter (i.e., translator) in Rome. Justin Martyr used Mark. Irenaeus and Clement of Alexandria agreed as to Mark's authorship. Opinions differ as to whether Mark wrote while Peter was alive. Papias and Clement both believed that Mark wrote under Peter's direction. This is the simplest view, since Justin includes Mark among "The Memoirs of the Apostles." The usage of Mark by the earliest Fathers is difficult to trace because about fifteen-sixteenths of Mark is also found in Matthew or Luke. Many quotations from Mark are identical with Matthew or Luke. Papias's witness, however, is positive and early. Clearly Mark was written for the Gentiles, probably the Romans to whom Peter ministered.

JOHN'S WRITINGS

The writings of John cover most of the rest of the New Testament. John, the beloved disciple, moved to Ephesus and lived to a great age. Polycarp knew him there. Patmos, the island of John's exile, was near Ephesus. Irenaeus, Polycarp's student, tells us that John lived until the days of Trajan (A.D. 98-117). Christians have always held dear the writings of John because they speak with such tender and intimate knowledge of Christ. They claim to be written by John "the beloved."

Their similar style strengthens the claim of each individual book. Both Clement of Rome and Ignatius refer to John's Gospel. Polycarp used 1 John. Papias probably knew John's Gospel, 1 John, and Revelation. Justin testified concerning John's Gospel and Revelation. The incomplete Muratorian Fragment cites by name John's Gospel, Revelation, and two epistles, probably 2 and 3 John. It also quotes 1 John 1:1. The testimony is quite sufficient.

An additional witness is now available. A small scrap of papyrus was discovered in Egypt in 1917 and published in 1931. Handwriting experts date this Rylands Papyrus at about A.D. 125, only thirty years or so after the death of John. This papyrus contains parts of five verses of John 18. Justin or Polycarp could even have seen it in their day.

In 1957 a more extensive papyrus of the Gospel of John was published. This Papyrus Bodmer II is dated about A.D. 200 and covers most of John's Gospel. It was a book, not a scroll, and only a few pages are missing. It is the earliest known extensive portion of the New Testament.

Later another similar papyrus was published, Bodmer XIV-XV, containing nearly all the Gospel of Luke and two-thirds of John bound together. It is possibly a little earlier than Papyrus Bodmer II. These were also books and are a precious early witness to the use and to the text of these Gospels.

PETER, JAMES, AND JUDE

The smaller epistles of Peter, James, and Jude have only limited witness in antiquity, but that witness is positive. Clement alludes to James, Polycarp to 1 and 2 Peter, Papias to 1 Peter. The Muratorian Fragment mentions Jude. Tertullian assures us that Jude was written by an apostle. Second Peter has strong internal testimony. It states that it is the second epistle by Peter, an apostle who witnessed Christ's transfiguration (1:1, 18; 3:1-2). It is of equally great interest that Jude (vv. 17-18) quotes from Peter's epistle and calls it the work of an apostle (2 Pet. 3:3). Another Papyrus Bodmer (VII-IX), dated before A.D. 300, is now available containing 1 and 2 Peter and Jude.

The identity of James and Jude, who were brothers (Jude 1), has been the subject of much discussion. There apparently were brothers James and Jude among the Twelve (Luke 6:16) and also brothers James and Jude who were half-brothers of the Lord (Matt. 13:55). Some scholars suggest that these half-brothers were really cousins of Christ and were identical with the James and Jude in the company of the Twelve. The evidence is perhaps indecisive, and it is not known which of the pairs, if there were two, wrote the epistles.

The dates these smaller epistles were written are not known. These and all other New Testament books were written by the apostles and their helpers "under the inspiration of the Spirit" as Clement of Rome says of Paul's letter to the Corinthians. Christian workers, leaders, and teachers should learn more about the time, authorship, and the circumstances related to all these epistles. Much can be learned by diligent study of the books themselves. The early authors confirm an intelligent faith in these books as the true, apostolic, and inspired Word of God.

No other books have been so widely considered, and we have no positive testimony that any other books were written by apostles. The early Fathers agree that some false writings were undoubtedly circulated (2 Thess. 2:2; 3:17). But these were promptly exposed, and only a few people were deceived. Though Christ never gave a list of New Testament books, He did appoint twelve apostles, then Paul, to be the foundation of the church. These men, divinely appointed and divinely endowed with the Spirit, wrote the New Testament of our Lord and Savior Jesus Christ. The Bible-believing Christian rejoices in this written Word of God.

VOCABULARY ENRICHMENT

Muratorian Fragment, *Didache* (pronounced di-da-kay).

DISCUSSION QUESTIONS

1. Make a table of the New Testament authors and their books.
2. By reviewing this chapter, verify the statement that "thirty years after the death of John only the single chapters of Jude and 2 John and 3 John are not attested in the works of the Fathers."
3. Who was Ignatius, and what of his writings do we have?
4. Who was the first Church Father whose writings remain?
5. Using 2 Peter 3:15-16 and Jude 17-18, explain the regard the apostles had for each other's words.
6. What proof is there that the apostles regarded their own works as inspired?
7. Trace the missionary journeys of Paul on a Bible map and list the order in which his epistles were written.
8. Why do we receive only twenty-seven books as the New Testament canon?

PRESERVATION OF THE BIBLE

New Testament

Most Christians have not thought seriously about how the New Testament writings were preserved. They can easily secure copies of the Bible and suppose that access to the Bible has always been available. Like all other blessings, however, this one should not be taken for granted. Men and women have died that the Bible might be preserved, translated, and published. Even in our day, in certain countries of the world, the Scriptures are scarce.

The history of the preservation of the New Testament can be divided into two periods—before the invention of the printing press and after. During the 1400s, three historical events were of inestimable benefit to the modern world. Columbus in 1492 discovered the New World, and America would become the world's cradle of liberty. Johann Gutenberg invented the printing press in 1456. And in 1493 Martin Luther, the founder of the Protestant Reformation, was born. These events have profoundly influenced the scope and effect of Christianity in modern times.

PRINTING THE BIBLE

The first book to come from Gutenberg's press was the Latin Bible. Copies of that first edition are preserved to this day. Soon afterward the Greek New Testament and the Hebrew Old Testament were both printed. Preserving the Scriptures after that became a relatively simple matter, for the Bible was produced by the thousands. After Tyndale translated the Bible into English, it was printed in Holland and smuggled into England. For a while the English bishops tried to burn all the copies, but they were unsuccessful. In a few years Tyndale's Bible and its successors were easily obtained all over England.

The opening verses of Genesis from the Gutenberg Bible, first published in 1456. Gutenberg's invention of movable type paved the way for distribution of the Bible in English seventy years later, with the publication of Tyndale's first edition of the New Testament in 1526.

Tyndale's translation of the opening words in Genesis, shown from a first edition of Tyndale's Pentateuch published in 1530.

After the printing press was invented, it became relatively easy to reproduce the Bible without mistakes. Previously, a person copied many pages by hand and was apt to make a few mistakes. If he discarded that work and started all over again, he probably would avoid those mistakes, but make others. Today in printing a book, it is a simple matter to correct any mistakes and leave the rest untouched. By careful proofreading, the Bible can be produced without any mistakes. In preparing plates for the printing of Bibles, the copy is proofread many, many times. Proofreaders may work in pairs, one reading from a correct copy and the other watching the proof sheets, or proofreaders may read through the copy while listening to an audio version of the Bible. In less expensive Bibles, there may be misprints because they are not so carefully checked. Most ordinary books are not so carefully proofread, and they are likely to have at least a few typographical errors.

Sometimes it was not a question of a mistake in copying, but rather of the style to be used. During the century after the 1611 King James Version was translated, a printer had to be a grammarian to know what spellings to change in successive reprints of the original King James Version.

For this reason, an old copy of the English Bible is different from recent editions. The differences are not mistakes or misprints. They reflect the practical adjustment of a changing language.

The KJV translation we use today is not an exact copy of that printed in 1611. Here is a reproduction of the original KJV with modern type but using the original spelling. An examination shows many strange forms and spellings that were modified throughout the first hundred years after it was published. For instance, "son" was spelled "sonne," "year" was "yeere," "he" was "hee," and music was "musick." The present-day Authorized Version contains all the changes made to approximately 1750.

The King James Version translation of the opening verses of Genesis, from a first edition of the King James Bible published in 1611.

EARLY COPIES

To comprehend how the New Testament was preserved, the student needs to understand the history of the ancient Roman Empire. In apostolic days the Roman Empire included the entire Mediterranean area—Spain, France, Italy, Greece, Turkey, Syria, Palestine, Egypt, and North Africa around Algiers. The empire also extended into Britain and parts of Germany. Latin was the government language, but most people used Greek.

Christianity was especially strong in Egypt, Palestine, Asia Minor, Rome, and North Africa. But Christianity was a forbidden religion, and at least ten different bitter persecutions broke out against its followers. Again and again Christian books were burned. Many Christians died rather than deliver their sacred books to the flames.

Finally Emperor Constantine the Great was converted in A.D. 313, after which he gave the famous Edict of Milan allowing freedom of religion. In succeeding decades, the Roman Empire weakened under attack from the barbarian Goths in Europe and from other peoples coming through Europe from Asia. In A.D. 410 Rome fell. Those were the days of Jerome, who made his Latin translation of the Bible called the Vulgate. Augustine was another leader whose name is still well known. Shortly after Rome fell, the empire was divided, with Constantinople as capital of the Eastern division and Rome as capital of the Western. The Eastern empire used Greek during the whole Middle Ages while the West used Latin.

The scholar who wants a New Testament as close as possible to that written by the apostles will treasure the Greek copies more than the Latin. Some early Greek copies date from before Jerome.

By God's providence, the student of the New Testament is favored in having many ancient copies. The original copies, called "autographs," were probably written on papyrus or leather scrolls. By A.D. 125, however, it was customary to use the form of the book called a codex, instead of a scroll. In this form it was easier to combine many writings into one volume. These books were copied and recopied in Greek. Before long, perhaps by A.D. 200, the church in Antioch and the area of Mesopotamia to the east wanted the Word in Syriac, its predominant language. Syriac is quite similar to Hebrew. By this time the church in North Africa wanted the Gospel in Latin; so an Old Latin translation was made. Later this translation was superseded by Jerome's Vulgate. Until A.D. 400, however, Greek continued to be the main biblical language.

Early copies of the New Testament were written in small letters. Medieval Greek manuscripts were also written this way. These copies are called "cursives." In the 300s it became the practice to make especially fine copies of the Bible on parchment, printed carefully in capital letters. These manuscripts are called "uncials," meaning capitals.

Several of these great uncial manuscripts have been preserved till today. For generations they were housed in the libraries of ancient monasteries, and only a few out of hundreds have withstood the ravages of time and waves of persecution. The latter was probably their worst enemy. When the Muslims invaded Egypt in the seventh century, they burned the great Alexandrian Library of 100,000 volumes, including the treasures of antiquity. About the same time, they burned the great Eusebian Library in Caesarea of Palestine with its treasures of early Christian antiquity. But in God's providence, many copies escaped the flames. It is said that there are about 3,000 copies of the Greek New Testament or parts of it. Of these, a dozen or more are over 1,500 years old.

THE OLD MANUSCRIPTS

What are our oldest manuscripts? What are they like? In the last two centuries, several important early manuscripts have been discovered. These manuscripts provide added information about the early text of the Bible.

The Alexandrian Text

In 1859 Constantine Tischendorf discovered a priceless manuscript among old works in the monastery of St. Catherine on the slopes of Mt. Sinai. This manuscript is called Codex Aleph, or Codex Sinaiticus, dating from the 300s of our era. Codex means book, not scroll, and Aleph is the first letter of the Hebrew alphabet.

In 1868 the Vatican Library published another old manuscript from the 300s called Codex B (sometimes called Vaticanus because it was found in the Vatican Library). These two manuscripts, Codex Aleph and Codex B, contain very similar wording, and it seems clear that they were copied from the same or similar master copies. They belong to the same family of manuscripts that has been called the Neutral Text, now better called the Alexandrian Text.

The Koine

Most copies made during the Middle Ages form another family of manuscripts differing in details of wording. It is called the Koine, meaning "common." It is also referred to as the *Textus Receptus*. This family was used by the King James translators. The Alexandrian Text was used by the Revised Version and Revised Standard Version committees. It is easy to compare these two families of manuscripts by comparing the King James Version and the Revised Versions of the New Testament. Most of the recent New Testament translations follow in general the Alexandrian Text, but the evidence for each questioned reading is usually considered afresh.

Other Manuscripts

In recent times even earlier copies have been found among piles of papyri unearthed in Egypt. The Chester Beatty Papyri cover much of the New Testament and come from the 200s.

The Rylands Papyrus, from about A.D. 125, is a valuable, though very small witness to the New Testament text. It is almost identical to the Alexandrian Text.

The Bodmer Papyri of John, also mentioned in chapter 5 in another connection, confirm the Alexandrian Text of that book. Most of the newer translations use these recently found manuscript readings.

TEXTUAL CRITICISM

The study of ancient manuscripts is called textual criticism, or lower criticism to distinguish it from destructive higher criticism. Textual criticism is an ancient, valuable study. It has been practiced by Christian scholars at least since Origen, of A.D. 250, but it must be done by those thoroughly trained in language. New Testament textual criticism has been put on a firmer basis since the work of Tischendorf, Westcott, Hort, and others.

Textual criticism can aid Christians in two ways. First, it can help to recover in most passages the very words written by the apostles. The copies presently available were made several generations after the originals were written. By comparing the testimony of the early families of manuscripts, the scholar can usually decide what words were originally written. Second, in some passages it is difficult to decide upon the original text. Did it say "Simon" or "Peter," "Jesus" or "Jesus Christ"? It may not be easy to decide, but when complete families of manuscripts agree, whichever wording is used, no great difference is involved.

It is usually held, on adequate evidence, that the Alexandrian family is closest to the original, though it must always be checked against other witnesses. And the Koine family, which most think to be more defective in detail, is still practically as good as our best. The differences only concern occasional details. The major differences between those modern translations done by believing scholars who made an earnest effort to translate accurately are not differences of the text families, but differences of interpretation and of wording. The remark of Westcott and Hort in 1881 is often quoted and is worth remembering:

> *If comparative trivialities . . . are set aside, the words in our opinion still subject to doubt can hardly amount to more than a thousandth part of the whole New Testament.*

More recent discoveries have confirmed and strengthened the conclusion of Westcott and Hort.

Our New Testament has been preserved by monk and scholar, by martyr and missionary, through laborious handwriting and by careful printing. In critical texts and numerous translations, the words of God by the apostles have been faithfully preserved and industriously spread over all the world. Christians may read and study their Bibles with confidence, knowing that this is the very Word of God.

"Heaven and earth shall pass away, but my words shall not pass away" (Matt. 24:35).

VOCABULARY ENRICHMENT

Autographs, cursives, text, textual criticism, uncials, Koine, *Textus Receptus*.

DISCUSSION QUESTIONS

1. How close is the date of the earliest New Testament manuscript segment to the life of its author, John?
2. What three great copies of the New Testament made before A.D. 400 are preserved in large portions?
3. Compare the resurrection narrative (John 20) in the King James and Revised Versions.
4. What basis do we have for confidence in even our poorest New Testament text?

7

PRESERVATION OF THE BIBLE

Old Testament

The Old Testament comes from a much earlier age than the New. Malachi, the last Old Testament book, was probably written about 400 B.C. Until recently, not much information has been available for the textual study of the Old Testament. However, the discovery of the Dead Sea Scrolls in 1947 provided a wealth of new textual material.

ANCIENT PRESERVATION

Moses and the other prophets wrote the Old Testament over a period of approximately 1,000 years—1400 B.C. to 400 B.C. During that time the sacred copies of the Scriptures were partly controlled by the temple priests, partly under the supervision of the king, and partly cared for by prophets to whom God gave His Holy Spirit for the revelation of His will. Prophecy was sometimes scarce in Israel, as in the days of Eli: "And the word of the LORD was precious in those days; there was no open vision" (1 Sam. 3:1). The nations often sank into idolatry, as in the days of Ahab. In all those periods, God raised up faithful prophets who were inspired by the Holy Spirit. These prophets loved and treasured the Word of God and gave it out courageously.

There is a lack of evidence about those times in Palestine from sources outside the Bible. However, the Bible contains internal evidence about its own composition and preservation. Secular literature, both writings and books, were doubtless composed during those days but have been lost. Multitudes of stories, histories, and poems are preserved on the imperishable clay tablets of Mesopotamia. In Egypt the writings were on papyrus, which, though fragile, has survived in that very dry climate. Traders from Palestine bought the Egyptian papyrus in exchange for cedar wood and olive oil. Papyrus was convenient for their use, but almost all these papyrus manuscripts perished in the rainy seasons of the hills of Palestine. Only in the hot, dry Dead Sea area have the ancient papyrus and leather scrolls been preserved. Thus the secular literature of Palestine was lost, and the biblical scrolls were worn out.

As the old scrolls were worn out or destroyed, they had to be recopied. What happened to these copies of the Bible after the last prophets finished their work in about 400 B.C.? Beginning at this end of history, we will work back to that ancient time 2,400 years ago.

An authentic Hebrew scroll opened to the beginning verses of Genesis

THE MIDDLE AGES

During the Middle Ages, the Hebrew Old Testament was preserved by the Jews. During that time, the lamp of learning in Europe burned very low. The Latin church used Jerome's Vulgate translation since none of its scholars seemed to know Hebrew. The Greek Orthodox Church in the Eastern Mediterranean area used the Greek Septuagint, and none of its theologians seemed to have paid any attention to the original Hebrew. And the Jews, despite cruel persecutions, spread everywhere and treasured their Scriptures and ancient customs and traditions.

Jewish tradition teaches that medieval rabbis copied the Scriptures with great care. They even counted the verses in a book and marked the middle verse. The result was a remarkably faithful transmission of the text.

Furthermore, when the Hebrew Bible is compared with the Latin translation made by Jerome in about A.D. 400 (the Vulgate), it is evident that Jerome worked with a Hebrew text much like the one in use today. Indeed, some translations were made into Greek in about A.D. 200 by various Jewish scholars. (These should not be confused with the Septuagint, which was made earlier.) These reveal that the Hebrew Bible of that day was close to present-day Hebrew. These "minor Greek translations" have not been preserved in their entirety, but even so, they help trace the history of the Hebrew text.

From before A.D. 200, however, there were no Hebrew copies until recently, and no important earlier translations were made until the Septuagint of 200 B.C. There was a Syriac, a Samaritan, and an Aramaic Targum, but their dates were uncertain, and they were relatively unimportant. There was, therefore, imperfect evidence for the careful preservation of the Hebrew text, at least before the year A.D. 200.

DEAD SEA SCROLLS

In 1947 an Arab shepherd threw a stone into a cave near the Dead Sea and heard the tinkle of breaking pottery. All the world now knows the story of the Bedouin who took seven manuscripts out of that cave, leaving hundreds of fragments. Since then other caves have yielded additional Old Testament manuscripts and related Jewish material. Thousands of fragments are still being patiently pieced together and studied. The Dead Sea Scrolls, buried long ago by the scribes of the sectarian community of Qumran, open up new and valuable evidence on the preservation of the Hebrew text in antiquity.

Nonbiblical Scrolls

The treasure includes two kinds of writings, the first of which are the nonbiblical scrolls. These writings show that the sect at Qumran regarded the books of the Old Testament as the product of God by His Spirit through the prophets. Repeatedly they refer to "the Law of Moses and the Prophets" or "what God spoke through Moses and all the Prophets." Their attitude toward the Old Testament and their terminology are similar to that of Christ and His apostles.

Biblical Scrolls

The second type of Dead Sea material is the biblical scrolls. These ancient copies of manuscripts have been compared directly with our Hebrew Bible. They demonstrate how accurately the ancient scribes did their work.

All the Old Testament books except one have been found in the caves. The book of Esther has not yet been identified. Some books, such as Psalms, Deuteronomy, and Isaiah, are represented in many copies. Others, such as Chronicles, are present only in fragments. The greatest scroll is Isaiah, preserved completely and in good condition. Apparently it can be dated at about 125 B.C. Some fragments are older. Portions of Job, Jeremiah, Samuel, and Psalms can be dated to 200 B.C. or earlier. One portion of Psalms is unofficially dated at about 300 B.C. A copy of Ecclesiastes dating from 150 B.C. is of special interest because some extreme critics have insisted that Ecclesiastes was written at a much later date. Copies of Daniel dating from the second century B.C. are significant because they are so close to the crucial date of 165 B.C. when critics claim the book was written.

Summary

The Dead Sea Scrolls are remarkably like our Hebrew Bible. They prove that those who copied the Hebrew Bible through all the years back to the second century before Christ did an extremely careful job. It is established that our Hebrew Bible in nearly its present form was used by the Jews 200 years before Christ, since some of the Dead Sea Scrolls are older than the Isaiah scroll. With confidence, it may be asserted that there is no known event in Israel's history that made any change in the Jews' habits of copying between Ezra's day and 200 B.C. Therefore, we conclude that the Old Testament is, in essentials and in detail, like the Scripture that Ezra caused to be read to the Jews in Jerusalem after his return from Babylonian captivity.

Such proof is enough for all ordinary purposes. However, today's scholars can trace the history of our Old Testament to an even earlier date. The Greek Septuagint, translated about 200 B.C., has been preserved in numerous copies made by Christian scribes, and an English translation has been made. Thus a student who does not know Greek and Hebrew can now compare the Septuagint with the King James Version. This is a great help, but it does raise some questions. The New Testament sometimes quotes from the Septuagint where the latter disagrees with the Hebrew. Is the Septuagint sometimes better than the Hebrew? Was this translation into the Greek done carefully?

Today there is positive evidence to answer these questions. Some Dead Sea manuscripts date from around 200 B.C. They are so much like the Septuagint that they represent the type of text used by the Septuagint translators. Where the Septuagint differs from our Hebrew, it is probably because there were already two or more different Hebrew texts running side by side as early as 200 B.C. The new evidence has solved several of the problems in New Testament quotations. It has shown that in these cases the Septuagint and the New Testament were undoubtedly right. It is remarkable that in all the centuries since then, these two types of texts have been preserved—one in Hebrew and the other in the Septuagint.

Of what value is a knowledge of the different "families" of Old Testament text? First, by careful comparison, the original reading can usually be determined. Second, the care with which the copiers handled all the texts in antiquity can be seen. Third, by comparing the two types as a whole, one can establish conclusively that neither text is far from the great early copies from which both families originated.

TEXTUAL COMPARISON

Two additional arguments reinforce the belief that the Old Testament has been copied with great accuracy from the earliest days. First, the passages of Scripture that quote each other agree quite closely. Second, the names appearing in both the Old Testament and in ancient inscriptions are in closest agreement. A few samples must suffice.

Agreement of Parallel Passages

There are more parallel passages in the Old Testament than most Bible readers realize. Psalm 18 is the same as 2 Samuel 22; Psalm 14 equals Psalm 53; Psalm 108 is made up of parts of Psalm 57 and Psalm 60. Isaiah 36—39 is the same as 2 Kings 18:13—20:19. Large parts of 2 Samuel and Kings are quoted in Chronicles.

Agreement of Names

Names provide an interesting "spot check." The Bible contains many complex names such as Shishak, Chedorlaomer, Azariah, Tiglath-Pileser, and Jehoiakim. Robert Dick Wilson stated that out of 184 letters of forty names preserved in our Hebrew copies, scarcely any are incorrectly preserved. Clay tablets found since Wilson's day have added other examples.

ANCESTRY OF THE ENGLISH BIBLE

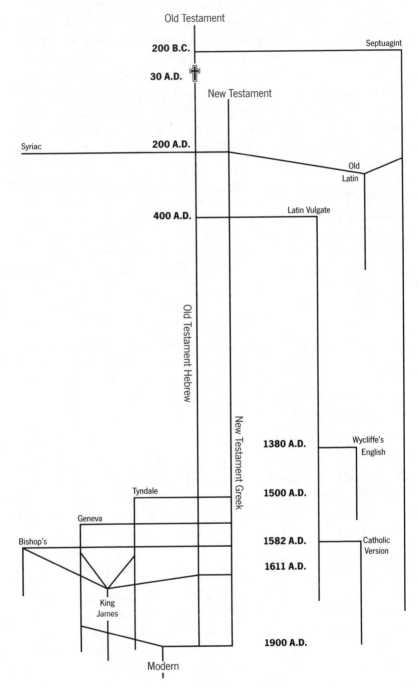

A striking example is Jeremiah 39:3. For centuries the men mentioned here were unknown. Recently the names of Nebuchadnezzar's officers have been found and can be checked with this verse. The names were confused with titles and were misread, but every letter was preserved accurately. It should read "Nergal-sharezer of Samgar,[1] Nebo-sarsechim the Rab-Saris, Nergal-sharezer the Rab Mag." Such accuracy in copying proves that the Old Testament text has been transmitted with marvelous fidelity. To all intents and purposes, the Bible student can affirm that the writings of the prophets have been preserved without any error that would affect the message of the Word of God. The text is reliable, and it may be used with the same confidence that was shown by Christ and the apostles.

Vocabulary Enrichment

Dead Sea Scrolls, external evidence, internal evidence, parallel passages, textual comparison, transmission, Vulgate.

Discussion Questions

1. How do we know that our Old Testament has been copied without any significant changes since A.D. 400? A.D. 200?
2. What is the Septuagint, and when was it made?
3. What two kinds of manuscripts were found in the caves around Qumran?
4. How many Old Testament books are represented among the Dead Sea Scrolls?
5. What are the approximate dates of some of the Old Testament scrolls and fragments?
6. How do the Dead Sea Scrolls show that the Old Testament was carefully copied in the centuries before Christ?
7. Compare the Septuagint text to today's Hebrew Old Testament.
8. What does textual criticism demonstrate about the Old Testament?
9. Read carefully 2 Samuel 22 and Psalm 18, noting the minor differences. Explain how slight alterations of the Hebrew text have caused this variation.
10. Prepare a display of pictures, written articles, and books that would show how the Old Testament was transmitted and preserved. Up-to-date encyclopedias, both secular and religious, contain explanatory articles and photographs of recent archeological finds. Make this display available to the entire Sunday school and church.

8

BIBLE PROBLEMS

The Bible is the most *important* book ever written. It is much larger than the average reader realizes. In ordinary-size type, without extensive notes, it covers about 1,300 pages. It is not surprising that skeptics and unbelievers find some problems in such a volume.

The Bible is a *strange* book—different from all other books. It deals with spiritual things that cannot be understood "naturally." Spiritual things are "spiritually discerned" (1 Cor. 2:14-16). Unfriendly critics, therefore, discover problems even where no real problems exist. Nicodemus exclaimed to Christ, "How can these things be?" (John 3:9). People unwilling to accept the Bible's spiritual message cannot understand it.

The Bible is an *ancient* book. It was written in Hebrew, Aramaic, and Greek by prophets, kings, tax gatherers, and scholars. Its historic setting changed from the Bronze Age to the Iron Age to Roman times. Its events occurred in Canaan, Egypt, Greece, and Asia Minor. No wonder it has puzzled some readers.

These supposed difficulties are the result of ignorance of Bible lands, customs, and languages. Most problems fade away under deep, earnest, and prayerful Bible study. The sincere Christian student should exercise faith and spiritual discernment.

The Bible contains remarkably few difficulties in comparison to its size and unusual background. The wonderful harmony of the book is a well-established fact. It was written over a period of sixteen centuries by approximately thirty-five authors. It tells one story and presents one consistent message. Its very harmony has been cited as one proof that it is inspired.

Some major classes of problems, however, have been raised. Several of these are related to miracles, prophecies, and the alleged contradictions of the Scriptures. In examining these, the student will discover the answers to other related problems and questions.

MIRACLES

Many miracles are recorded in the Bible. Some affected large areas and many people—like the crossing of the Red Sea (Exod. 14). Some were smaller, less conspicuous—such as Elisha making an iron axe head float (2 Kings 6:1-7). Some were healings—Jesus healing the blind man (John 9). Others were in the realm of nature—Jesus feeding five thousand with a few loaves and fishes (Mark 6:34-44).

How important are these miracles? What do they teach? Can twenty-first-century Christians believe them? How? Why? In order to answer these questions, we must know what biblical miracles are.

All biblical miracles had one thing in common: They were related to the natural world. Iron floated, water turned into blood, leprosy was healed, deafness was cured, lame men walked, storms were stopped.

Biblical miracles were also unusual events, contrary to ordinary experience. They were unbelievable and impossible for mere man to accomplish. People do not walk on water. Iron does not float. Fire does not come down from heaven and lick up a sacrifice—water, stones, and all. Miracles resulted from direct intrusion by supernatural powers. A miracle is a remarkable event in the natural world, totally beyond man's ability to produce.

Today it is popular to deny the possibility of miracles. David Hume argued that it would take infinite evidence to prove that miracles exist. Scientists insist that fixed laws govern the universe, and no exceptions are possible. They maintain that ancient, unenlightened, gullible people believed that God ran the universe directly and could easily change anything He wanted to. Some scientists say, "We know that God—if there be a God—operates through regular natural laws that admit to no exception."

The Bible clearly shows, however, that early peoples were not gullible. True, they did not have scientific data, but they knew that people could not walk on water (Matt. 14:25; Mark 6:49; John 6:19). When they saw Christ so doing, they were terrified and thought He was a ghost. When Paul healed the lame man (Acts 14), the people were convinced that the gods had appeared in the likeness of men. They knew that mere human power could not do this. The blind man whom Jesus healed said, "Since the world began was it not heard that any man opened the eyes of one that was born blind" (John 9:32). He knew that Jesus had done something that was impossible for mere man to do.

The science of that day was elementary, but the people believed in the regularity of nature and in the law of cause and effect. They believed the miracles not because they were gullible, but because the sensory evidence was inescapable. They believed that the God of miracles had entered this sinful world in His own revealing power.

Some critics have gone to great lengths to discredit the miracles. They suggest that Jesus healed by psychology, that the disciples did not see Him on the water but on the reeds near the shore. The feeding of the five thousand is explained away by assuming that the people had brought their lunches, and the lad's unselfish example had shamed them into sharing with each other. Such unscientific, foolish theories found in many modernistic books do not deal with the plain evidence in the case.

The crowning miracle of all, Christ's resurrection, is totally unexplainable by natural means (Matt. 28; Mark 16; Luke 24; John 20). The strongest argument for His bodily resurrection is the transformation Christ wrought in the disciples. Those who had forsaken and fled (Mark 14:50) became bold witnesses, ready to die for their faith.

Those who explain away the miracles, including Christ's resurrection, have nothing left but empty religion without power, joy, or salvation—a vain philosophy without God's blessed revelation. Theirs is the darkness of midnight without the light of life. True Christians have no problem with miracles. Miracles are at the heart of the Christian's faith. Their reality as recorded in God's Word is a final, exclusive proof of the validity of Christian hope and confidence.

Paul had the answer for all skepticism. When he appeared before Festus and Agrippa, the governor refused to believe Paul's doctrine. He declared that Paul was mad (Acts 26:24). Paul's answer to Agrippa was a sober argument: "Why should it be thought a thing incredible with you, that God should raise the dead?" (Acts 26:8). Anyone who believes God has no difficulty accepting miracles. The consistent, sensible, merciful miracles of the New Testament are proof that the merciful God has spoken indeed. Miracles are an essential witness to, and proof of, our faith.

Prophecies

The argument from prophecy is equally striking. Bible prophecy includes definite, positive, often long-range predictions that no observer could expect, no matter how wise. Of course, shrewd observers can predict certain things. The weatherman attempts a limited forecast. Political "pollsters" attempt to predict election results weeks in advance. But true predictive prophecy is supernatural.

Old Testament Fulfillment

Bible prophecies were not double-tongued predictions like those of the Greek oracles. A Greek oracle predicted that if a certain king would fight, he would destroy a great empire. He did so. The empire he destroyed was his own. In contradistinction, Hebrew prophets foretold the future with definiteness, often predicting the dates and the names of the participants. The prophets spoke because God gave them supernatural insight and detailed information about future things. This is one of the vital proofs of the entire Bible's authenticity. Every evangelical Christian believes this truth.

How do skeptics treat these prophecies? Very cleverly. When a chapter in Isaiah predicts Cyrus's reign, they say, "That chapter was written after Cyrus came to the throne." If the books of Kings predict Josiah by name, they erroneously teach that "Josiah's name was slipped into the verse by a later copyist after Josiah arose." If Daniel predicts the days of Antiochus Epiphanes, that is held to be positive proof that Daniel was written after 165 B.C. The liberal scholars' attitude toward predictive prophecy is the reason they insist that the Old Testament was written at a later date and by authors other than the books allege.

What is the answer to such objectionable criticism? First, the bias against supernaturalism must be pointed out. Next, it can be shown that both internal and external evidence favor the earlier dating. Among the Dead Sea Scrolls are copies of Daniel made in about 110 B.C. that prove that Daniel could not have been written by a false Daniel in a hoax at about 165 B.C. It could hardly have been copied and recopied widely and its false origin kept hidden and its canonical authority recognized all in the space of fifty-five years. The Dead Sea material strongly supports the earlier date for Daniel, and that makes Daniel predictive prophecy.

Second, many Bible prophecies refer to the first coming of Christ or to events during this age that happen long after any possible date for the prophetic utterance. Many instances could be cited. The prophecy of the virgin birth of Christ is a case in point (Isa. 7:14). Critics say that the word means "young woman" and referred to Isaiah's son soon to be born or to an expected child of Ahaz. In the context this child, Immanuel, is also called "Wonderful," and is promised to be of David's line (Isa. 9:6-7). Isaiah already had a son, Shearjashub, so the passage could not refer to him. Nor could it apply to Ahaz's son, Hezekiah, who by this time was over nine years old. Hezekiah was twenty-five when he succeeded Ahaz, and Ahaz had reigned for sixteen years. As further proof, the word *virgin*, used six other times in the Old Testament, is never applied to a married woman. At least three times it clearly means a virgin. Further, the Septuagint translation uses a word specifically meaning "virgin." Long before Christ's birth, the Jews accepted this clear prophecy of the Virgin Birth. Only critical bias prevents the acceptance of this great prediction.

Consider Daniel's prophecy of the seventy weeks (Dan. 9:24ff.). It plainly says that from the time of the commandment being given to build Jerusalem to the coming of Messiah the Prince shall be seven weeks and sixty-two weeks, and after the sixty-second week the Messiah shall be cut off, and the city shall be destroyed. Critical scholars have unsuccessfully attempted a different translation of this passage and have dissolved its meaning by claiming that the time periods are only symbolic.

Two explanations should be noted. First, the word *week* refers to a unit of seven years as observed by the Jews. The Hebrews counted time in sevens and fifties—weeks and jubilees. Debts were to be forgiven after seven years, and everyone was to go back to his family holdings in the fiftieth Year of Jubilee. The practice was as old as the Levitical legislation. The intertestamental *Book of Jubilees* dates events in Genesis by their jubilee, week, year, month, and day. Obviously, "week" means a seven-year period. Seven and sixty-two weeks are therefore sixty-nine weeks of years, or 483 years. An additional week mentioned in verse 27 accounts for the total of seventy.

Second, there were various commandments to restore and rebuild Jerusalem. The first one was by Cyrus about 539 B.C. This was later revoked, and only the temple was built. The next such decrees were in the time of Ezra and Nehemiah, between 456 B.C. and 444 B.C. Ezra 9:9 implies that Ezra's decree included building Jerusalem. So Ezra rebuilt the city, and his friend Nehemiah finished the wall. Some therefore count from Nehemiah's date, using years slightly shorter than usual (because Revelation 11:2 compared with 12:6 refers to years 360 days long). It seems more natural to use normal years such as the Jews regularly used and count from Ezra's date. Thus 456 B.C. minus 483 years equals A.D. 26. (There is no 0 year, so the result is not A.D. 27.) This is exactly when Christ was announced by John the Baptist as the Messiah of Israel. Shortly afterward this Messiah was cut off. Forty years later the city was destroyed in a bitter siege by the Romans. On any theory of the dating of Daniel, the prophecy, strictly interpreted, refers to events long after Daniel. The argument from prophecy thus is strong here.

Opinions may differ as to the fulfillment of the seventieth week.

Premillennialists (of whom the writer is one) believe that it remains to be fulfilled in accordance with the indications given by Christ in Matthew 24:15ff.

New Testament Fulfillment

Many New Testament predictions are being fulfilled today. Jesus made a bold prediction when He told a few fishermen, "the gospel must first be published among all nations" (Mark 13:10). Yet from its small beginning, the Christian church has grown to cover all the major areas in the world. Jesus also predicted, "This generation [NIV footnote—nation] will certainly not pass away until all these things have happened" (Matt. 24:34). The Jews have persisted even when they were dispersed, persecuted, outlawed, and massacred. Their present return to Palestine is a further vital fulfillment of ancient prophecies (Zech. 12:1ff.).

These predictions are neither a problem nor an embarrassment to personal Christian faith. The abundance of fulfilled prophecies is a supernatural proof that God has spoken.

ALLEGED CONTRADICTIONS

Liberals charge that there are a number of contradictions in the Bible. These are not as serious as the critics affirm. It is impossible in this study to answer all of them. John Haley surveyed the literature of modern criticism and reviewed all the difficulties that they mentioned. His carefully prepared answers have been accepted because of their faithfulness to the facts. They are worthy of consideration. Additional suggestions have been made by other evangelical scholars.

One such alleged contradiction is Judas's suicide. Matthew 27:5 reports, "He . . . went and hanged himself." Acts 1:18 says, "And falling headlong, he burst asunder in the midst." The original word translated "hanged" in Matthew does not necessarily refer to hanging, but to suicide in general or to strangling. It is used in 2 Samuel 17:23 to translate the Hebrew *hanaq*, a root used only in Nahum 2:12 and Job 7:15 to mean not specifically "hang" but any kind of strangulation. Death by hanging was not common in Old Testament times. Of course, if Judas's body was undiscovered, it would bloat and burst. The alleged contradiction may be due to over-precise translation.

Mark 14:30 and 72 record Peter's threefold denial before the cock crowed twice. The other Gospels refer only to the cock crowing. Some of the oldest manuscripts of Mark do not include the word *twice*, thus agreeing with Matthew and Luke. In 2 Chronicles 36:9, Jehoiachin was eight years old when carried captive, but 2 Kings 24:8 says he was eighteen. Some Hebrew texts and the Greek Septuagint translation say eighteen years old in both places. This was clearly the original reading in both books. Textual criticism solves this problem.

Another example is that of the blind man healed as Jesus was leaving Jericho (Mark 10:46-52). Parallel accounts seem to disagree. Matthew 20:30 reads, "And, behold, two blind men sitting by the way side." Luke 18:35 mentions "a certain blind man" healed as Jesus came near Jericho, meaning that he was healed in the vicinity of Jericho. At that time there were two Jerichos—the old city and the one housing Herod's winter palace. The company of disciples could be leaving the one city and in the vicinity of the other. These accounts are not contradictory; one simply tells more than the others.

Many other supposed contradictions are not contradictory narratives, but rather are supplementary accounts. The inscription over the cross is of this nature, with slight variations in the four Gospels. The inscription was in Greek, Latin, and Hebrew. Other trilingual inscriptions from those days were not identical in all languages. The variation indicates that one Gospel gave part of the title; others gave additional parts.

Most alleged contradictions are not serious. A good reference Bible often suggests answers. The problems usually lie in our limited knowledge or misinterpretation of the situation.

Skeptical minds overemphasize the problems in the Bible. In spite of their assaults, the Bible stands, and multitudes of ordinary Christians and faithful scholars find in it the light of life and the truth of God. We should remember Peter's confession of faith: "Lord, to whom shall we go? thou hast the words of eternal life" (John 6:68). Many people turn back because of the difficult sayings of Christ, but "we believe and are sure that thou art that Christ, the Son of the living God" (John 6:69).

THE BIBLE AND SCIENCE

The idea is abroad that modern scientific advances make it impossible to believe the Bible. This is not true for the Bible believer who really studies the Word. The Bible is inspired and is true not only in spiritual matters, but also when it touches science and history. It is not a textbook on science. It seldom bears on physics, chemistry, mathematics, or electricity. The major conflict between the Bible and science is in the first chapters of Genesis, usually relating to evolution. This controversy revolves mainly around three subjects: the great antiquity of the earth, the fixity of species, and the origin of man.

The Antiquity of the Earth

Geology claims that the earth is four or five billion years old. How does this fit the Bible? Only the briefest answer is possible. Some Bible scholars have suggested that the six creative days are really long periods of time and not literal twenty-four-hour days. The first three "days" occurred before the sun was set to mark time.

Those holding this view also suggest that these days need not be of equal extent. The first may have been extremely long. The creation of plant life, the final phases of formation of the sun and moon, and the beginning of animal life could have occurred fairly close together, followed by a long period of growth and further creation.

On the other hand, other Bible scholars holding to the literal six twenty-four-hour days of creation argue that God could have created the world with the appearance of age. It must be clear that the Bible is true regarding the antiquity of the earth.

The Fixity of Species

In this problem much depends on the meaning of the word *species*. There is no all-embracing definition. In biology species are identified as *plants or animals having similar characteristics*. As thus defined, species are not fixed. For instance, cabbage, cauliflower, and brussels sprouts look very different, and yet they interbreed freely. If we define species, however, as *organisms that interbreed with each other but not with other species*, then the species is fixed, with only rare examples of crossing over the species boundary.

The Age of Man

There has been no established figure on how long human beings have been on the earth. Older theories of evolution had held that primitive humans appeared during the Glacial Period, the so-called Pleistocene, some 500,000 years ago. They were followed by Neanderthal man about 60,000 years ago and by Cro-Magnon man only 25,000 years ago. These theories have changed through recent discoveries. Carmel man was discovered with some modern characteristics, though he was dated to about 125,000 years ago by glacial correlations. That dating has more recently been changed to 35,000 by the carbon-14 method, which itself still has considerable uncertainty. The Swanscombe man and Kanjera man were discovered with many modern characteristics, though they were dated to 300,000 years ago. The date, based also on glacial phenomena, is quite questionable. Scientists now agree that the Neanderthals were not so primitive as formerly believed. The whole subject of dating by science is undependable and is constantly being restudied.

New discoveries in these fields are coming rapidly with the finds of Louis Leakey in Olduvai Gorge, Africa, and his son, Richard Leakey, farther north, Donald Johanson, and others. Although the cited ages of these creatures is excessive (two or three million years old), the earliest specimens claimed by Richard Leakey have an upright stature, human-like tooth structure, and tool-making ability. The evidence here may be for variation within the human race, but not evolution.

The Bible itself, while being definite about the facts of creation, gives no specific dates for creation. Most Bible scholars, however, believe in a young creation, perhaps only ten to fifteen thousand years old.

Growing experience with Scripture and a sincere faith in its divine origin will lead the student to a deep confidence that, when all the facts are known, *true* science will be in harmony with a sober, careful, strict interpretation of the Bible.

VOCABULARY ENRICHMENT

Alleged contradictions, critical bias, evolutionary theory, miracle, science.

DISCUSSION QUESTIONS

1. Identify the eight nonhealing miracles in the Gospels.
2. How can the devil and his minions perform miracles (cf. Exod. 7:22; Rev. 13:14)?
3. Read Peter's sermon in Acts 2 and Paul's sermon in Acts 13 and list the prophecies that are fulfilled in Christ.
4. In the light of modern science, give reasons why Christians can continue to believe the Bible.
5. State some contradictions not covered in this chapter that you may have discovered. How can these problems be answered?

9

HIGHER CRITICISM AND THE BIBLE

All Bible students should learn something about the attacks that have been leveled against the Bible. By so doing, they will be prepared to try the spirits and be able to resist being led away by those who are unstable and distort the Scripture to their own destruction (2 Pet. 3:16). Similarly, a medical student studies diseases in order to learn how to keep people healthy.

There have always been people who disbelieve the Bible. In our day there is a particular type of unbelief expressed in *higher criticism*. We need not study all the details of this viewpoint, but it is wise to know that such criticism does exist.

DEFINITION

Higher criticism includes the study of the date and authorship of Bible books. Many higher critics hold that some or all of the books of the Bible were not written by the men that the books claim as authors, that the books were not written when they claim to be written, and that they were often not unified books but composed of several documents pieced together.

Today some orthodox scholars use the term higher criticism in a somewhat different sense. They admit there is a place for the right kind of higher criticism, something altogether different from the vicious, unbelieving higher criticism of the liberals. Orthodox higher critics study the authorship and background of Bible books. They use the techniques of higher criticism, but they do it reverently. The orthodox type of higher criticism is merely another name for what has been called "Bible introduction."

The phrase "higher criticism" usually refers to the unbelieving type outlined above. It has been and is destructive of faith and is fatal to Christian endeavor. If the Bible is a mass of falsehood (as the liberal critics teach), why read it at home or preach it abroad? Why teach our children to keep the Ten Commandments if the commandments themselves bear false witness to Moses' experience with God on Sinai?

In order to understand this erroneous theory, it is necessary to review certain historical backgrounds. In 1753 a French physician, Jean Astruc, noticed that the name for the deity in the book of Genesis is sometimes "God" (Hebrew, *Elohim*) and sometimes "Jehovah" or *YHWH* (LORD in the King James Version). Astruc suggested that the variation was the result of Moses' having used two different sources when he composed Genesis, one called an "E source" and the other a "J source." Astruc did not deny that Moses was the author, but he concluded that these two sources woven together make up our book of Genesis.

Old Testament Criticism

Later writers in the rationalistic era of French and German thought extended Astruc's theory and said that the Pentateuch was actually the work of someone much later than Moses. "E" was said to be the early document and "J" the later.

In 1853 Hupfeld of Germany turned things around. He declared that the "E" document was itself made up of two parts, one of which was very late. Later German critics, especially Wellhausen (1878), went further and claimed that they could find four documents in the Pentateuch. Their names and dates are:

J   document, 850 B.C. (now placed a bit earlier—named from the use of "Jehovah" for Lord)

E   document, 750 B.C. (named from the use of "Elohim" for God)

D   document, 625 B.C. (largely made up of Deuteronomy)

P   document, 450 B.C. (having a major priestly emphasis)

Wellhausen held that none of the Pentateuch was written by Moses and presumed that the whole record of the priestly or sacrificial system had been compiled by men living 1,000 years after Moses.

Mosaic Authorship of the Pentateuch

Higher criticism does not stop with denying the Mosaic authorship. It denies also the truth and value of the Pentateuch. It declares that there never was any wilderness tabernacle. It holds that those stories were made up by postexilic priests.

Some of the early critics even declared that Moses did not know how to write—if there was a Moses. They called the histories of the patriarchs "a mass of later legend." The exodus from Egypt was often doubted completely (Exod. 12ff.). The Sinai legislation was called spurious (Exod. 20ff.). The miracles of the ten plagues (Exod. 7:9ff.), crossing the Red Sea (Exod. 14:21ff.), giving of manna (Exod. 16:14ff.), and others were all explained away. More serious yet was the higher critics' denial that God had revealed Himself to early people as the true, holy, and only God. Higher critics insisted that the patriarchs in Abraham's day were crude *animists* (worshipers of stones and trees); by Moses' day they were *polytheists* (worshipers of many gods); David was a *henotheist* (the belief that every nation had its own particular God); *monotheism* (belief in one God) was the discovery of the eighth-century prophets. This diabolical reconstruction of Israel's early religion and history was the "fully assured result" of German rationalistic criticism at the beginning of the twentieth century. To deny this view was to be labeled as backward and ignorant of the facts. Thank God, many thousands of Bible-believing Christians never surrendered to the subtle attacks of the liberal higher critics.

David, Isaiah, and Daniel

Higher criticism went far beyond the Pentateuch. It was inevitable that the entire Word of God should be discounted. If David was not a monotheist, he could not have written the psalms, for they speak of one holy, living, and true God. For these and other reasons, the critics set the writing of most of the Old Testament books at a later date. Isaiah was supposed to have been written by one, two, three, or more men. They say that Isaiah did not predict the coming of Cyrus 175 years in advance. It was the writing of Deutero-Isaiah, or a second Isaiah, who lived during Cyrus's time. They also claim that Daniel did not predict the succession of the great empires of Babylon, Medo-Persia, and Greece down to Antiochus Epiphanes in 165 B.C. The book was presumed written at a later time when Antiochus Epiphanes was fighting the Maccabees, and it was actually ancient history instead of the prophecy it pretended to be. Thus the higher critics did not limit their destruction to the structural details of the text. They struck at the very basic truth and value of almost every Old Testament book.

Christ's Approval of the Old Testament

Higher criticism affects our view of both the Old Testament and the New. It is quite clear, as studied in chapter 2, that Christ and the apostles fully believed the Old Testament. Jesus taught that "it is easier for heaven and earth to pass, than one tittle of the law to fail" (Luke 16:17). He declared that the Old Testament was more convincing than if one should rise from the dead (Luke 16:29-31). He believed the historical reality of Adam and Eve, Jonah and the huge fish, the manna from heaven, and all the other Old Testament events. Christ was not a higher critic. Modern criticism, therefore, pictures Christ as a person of His time, subject to the simple, noncritical, erroneous teaching of His day. Liberal critics teach that He gradually became aware of His Messiahship, was mistaken about His second coming, and died not as the divine substitute (1 Pet. 2:24-25) but as a human martyr. Higher criticism strips the Old Testament of its value and robs the New Testament of its Lord.

And, sad to say, this view has become widespread and deeply entrenched. It is the very basis of what is often called modernism. In the early days of the twentieth century, promising young theologians went to Europe to take advanced training and often came back infected with the modernistic teachings of the German learning. Most of the older, larger theological schools accepted this liberalism as the basis of their theological teaching, and their graduates for years preached these ideas. Most local Christian workers and leaders can hardly realize the extent of this influence. It has been resisted by the Bible institutes and Bible colleges and by a goodly number of orthodox, evangelical colleges and seminaries, especially those seminaries founded after 1920. But it has affected a large percentage of the Protestant preachers of our generation. The effects of higher criticism should be thoroughly understood by every Christian worker and Sunday school teacher.

THE OLD CRITICISM

The hallmarks of the older liberal higher criticism are references to the J, E, D, P documents, the denial of the unity of Isaiah, the holding of a late date (after the exile) for most of the psalms, the Maccabean date of Daniel (165 B.C.), the idea of the evolution of Israel's religion (rather than its revelation), the discovery of monotheism by eighth-century-B.C. prophets, and many similar denials. By logic and in point of fact, a person who believes part of higher criticism believes other parts too. One who believes in "two or three Isaiahs" will hardly believe that Daniel was written in 550 B.C. One who believes that Moses did not write anything will also refuse to believe that David wrote the psalms attributed to him. Higher criticism is a system, and at every basic point it is opposed to orthodox Christianity.

Fortunately, higher criticism itself is under attack today. In the providence of God there have been remarkable archeological discoveries since about 1920. These have convinced scholars, even many of the unorthodox, that the histories of Genesis are true, that Moses may well have been monotheistic, that many psalms were written as early as David. According to a very prominent scholar, W. F. Albright, the old Wellhausen theory has suffered a "total breakdown." The old positions are being greatly modified. The new archeological discoveries actually support the old orthodox position. However, not many are suddenly returning to orthodoxy. Instead, they are propounding new types of critical views that have not been accepted by all scholars. These are just as wrong as the earlier views.

The New Criticism

The newer criticism is not as unified as critical views were earlier in the twentieth century, and it cannot be followed out in detail. There is an oral tradition theory that holds that nothing was written down until exilic times, but all of Israel's traditions were passed on orally. A more usual view holds substantially to the documentary theory of the J, E, D, and P sources but tries to trace the oral traditions behind such sources. Other views subdivide the sources into J1, J2, P^A, P^B, etc. A common view now holds that the documents J, E, and P can be traced only through Genesis, Exodus, Leviticus, and Numbers (the so-called Tetrateuch) and that the "Deuteronomist" author, editor, or school wrote Deuteronomy, Joshua, Judges, Samuel, and Kings at a time near the exile. Of course the work of the Deuteronomist is not a unit. He used older material, and much has been inserted into his work, according to these scholars, in the later days.

The arguments for these views are quite subjective, which is why they can be so diverse. They begin with the old arguments used by Wellhausen about parallel passages, contradictory statements, and characteristic wordings and concepts and proceed to divide the text as these hints impress them. It is interesting that the extent of the P document in Genesis, for instance, as given by Driver almost a century ago agrees rather closely with the view held today by Martin Noth[1]. The main difference is that Noth finds no P document in Genesis 14 and 24. Genesis 14 was called quite late, even Maccabean (i.e., about 165 B.C.) by early critics.

Today archeological study has shown that it fits the times of the patriarchs and no later. That the belief in the J, E, D, and P documents is still held so persistently and with little change is surprising, since no archeological discovery has given evidence of such documents. On the contrary, many finds have supported the historicity of these biblical texts in major and in minor matters. For further study of the complicated details of these critical analyses, see the works of Archer, Allis, Unger, and Young listed in the Resources for Enrichment section at the end of this text.

VOCABULARY ENRICHMENT

Animist, evangelical, henotheist, higher criticism, liberalism, monotheist, orthodox, polytheist.

DISCUSSION QUESTIONS

1. Mention several interrelated ideas of higher criticism in connection with Old Testament books.
2. Give several reasons why higher criticism is harmful to the Christian faith.
3. Explain what higher criticism believes in regard to predictive prophecy and the reality of miracles.
4. What modern factor is helping to disprove the old higher criticism?

10

ARCHEOLOGY AND THE OLD TESTAMENT

Volumes have been written on the relationship of archeology to the Old Testament. In this chapter, it is impossible to do more than define archeology, show the limits of its study, and demonstrate how it bears on the Old Testament.

DEFINITION

Archeology is "the study of ancient things." For all practical purposes, it is limited to that study of ancient history that is illuminated by the digging up of buried cities, tombs, and other relics. Biblical archeology is mainly concerned with the archeology of Palestine, Egypt, and Mesopotamia.

Archeologists proceed by carefully digging up ancient remains, photographing, recording everything exactly as found, and interpreting the results. They also translate and study the documents produced.

HISTORY

In the Middle Ages, the paintings and writings in Egyptian temples were thought to be magical. In about 1700 archeologists discovered the Rosetta Stone, written in three languages, including Greek. This gave scholars the key to the Egyptian language.

In the 1800s, the Behistun inscription of Darius the Great was deciphered. This inscription was also in three languages and gave the key to the Assyrian-Babylonian language. Scholars now call this the Akkadian language, after the city of Akkad mentioned in Genesis 10:10. The Akkadian language was written by using a wedge-shaped stick to make various combinations of marks on soft clay tablets usually about the size and shape of a bar of soap. These tablets were then sun-dried and are often beautifully preserved. This writing is called cuneiform (wedge-shaped).

In Palestine and Egypt most of the writing was done on papyrus, a paperlike material made from the papyrus plant. Papyrus rots quickly in the damp rainy season of the Palestinian winter, so only a little writing has been preserved in Palestine. An exception is the recent discovery of many leather scrolls and fragments in the caves of the hot, dry Dead Sea district. These scrolls date from about 200 B.C. to A.D. 50. Aside from these, Palestinian writing is restricted to a few inscriptions, seals, and writings on pottery.

Early archeologists were unskilled and unscientific in their approach. They dug through the ancient ruins in accidental fashion, hoping to find written material, well-preserved statues, or other treasure. They finally discovered that the ancient cities of Palestine and Mesopotamia were built in layers, one on top of another. The earliest cities were abandoned in time of war, famine, or pestilence. The mud-brick houses and walls tumbled down. Later new groups of settlers moved in, leveled out the old ruins, and built a new level right on top. As many as twenty-three layers or cities have been found on a single location. Later archeologists uncovered the strata in excavation sites one by one. Thus they could get the relationships of one group of inhabitants to another.

The study of archeology grew slowly until World War I. About that time, archeologists realized that the layers of each period were marked by characteristic types of pottery. A careful examination and study of the types of objects, especially pottery, made it possible to compare the layers of one city with the layers of cities uncovered in other locations. Further comparison with occasional inscriptions allowed these layers to be dated, often very accurately. It is therefore said that archeology became a science in about 1920. Archeological works older than that may have contained valuable facts, but they had to be restudied by the more accurate procedures and methods of later archeology.

The advances of archeology in the past half-century have been tremendous. A hundred years ago, little was known about the history of Egypt, Mesopotamia, or Palestine before 800 B.C. Now there are brilliant illuminations back to 3,000 B.C. and earlier. Scientists know the names of the ancient kings of Babylon, Assyria, and Egypt. These kings are also mentioned in the Bible, and the names and even the pictures of some of them have been discovered. Ancient battles, laws, languages, and cultures have come to life under patient investigation.

What bearing has this had upon the Bible itself? Naturally, a great deal. Recent discoveries have confirmed and illuminated the Bible and in many cases have effectively answered Bible critics.

CONFIRMATION

Many parts of the Old Testament cannot yet be confirmed. No archeologists can prove that "The Lord is my shepherd, I shall not want." Archeology is concerned with Bible history. It can confirm facts in the historical and prophetical books, but it cannot bring spiritual discernment.

Archeological discoveries have confirmed Shishak's war against Rehoboam (1 Kings 14:25-26), the kingship of Omri and the power of Ahab (1 Kings 16:22), the rebellion of Mesha of Moab (2 Kings 3:5), the fall of Samaria (2 Kings 18:10), the digging of Hezekiah's tunnel (2 Kings 20:20), the invasion of Pharaoh-Nechoh (2 Kings 23:29), the fall of Jerusalem and the deportation of Jehoiachin (2 Kings 24:10-15).

It is most striking when some detail long forgotten by everyone, except the Bible authors, is confirmed. Such proven conclusions argue that the books of the Bible were written by eyewitnesses or by other men who knew the facts intimately and who lived in the age concerned. Two examples are sufficient for illustration.

Baruch's Seal

Baruch, Jeremiah's scribe, was doubtless a minor personage. No one but a contemporary would know about him. He is not mentioned outside of the book of Jeremiah where his name occurs twenty-three times in chapters 32, 36, 43, and 45. But in Jerusalem a seal was discovered with the inscription: "Belonging to Baruch, son of Neriah, the Scribe." In the same cache, a seal was found with the inscription "Belonging to Jerahmeel, son of the King" (cf. Jer. 36:26, 32). The most natural conclusion is that the book of Jeremiah was written by a contemporary.

The Ironsmiths

A different type of illustration is found in 1 Samuel 13:19-21 where the Philistines did not allow the Israelites to have smiths, lest the Israelites make themselves swords. This passage had long been difficult to translate. It seemed odd that there were no Hebrew "smiths," since metalworking had existed for centuries all over the Near East. Later information proves that these verses reflect accurately the situation in Israel just at that time. The Philistines introduced the Iron Age into Palestine and at first maintained a strict monopoly on iron-working. There were no ironsmiths in Israel, for the Philistines kept iron-working a military secret.

The phrase "They had a file for the mattocks" is now illustrated by the discovery of a weight inscribed with a form of the word translated "mattock." Evidently this word does not mean "mattock," but refers to the price charged for sharpening agricultural tools. The knowledge of such a detail is clear proof that the author of 1 Samuel was in full possession of his facts. Later copyists who did not know the complete picture misinterpreted the verse. We now see what the original author meant. Thus we can translate the Hebrew word correctly.

ILLUMINATION

Other examples can be given of the use of archeology in illustrating and illuminating the Old Testament. These confirm the Bible and show the background against which it should be fitted. Illumination is important, however, in its own right, because the Bible cannot be fully appreciated until it is understood. Adequate knowledge will save the student from many serious errors of interpretation. Here again only a few scattered illustrations can be given.

The Horites

A group of people called Horites or Horims are mentioned in Genesis, Numbers, and Deuteronomy and were apparently connected with Edom. The Horites seem to have been related to the Jebusite dwellers in Jerusalem. The word *hor* in Hebrew means "hole." For this reason, one of the standard older lexicons (a book containing an alphabetical arrangement of the words in a language, with the definition of each), such as the one by Brown, Driver, and Briggs, stated that the name Horite "probably equals cave-dweller." This statement implies that there was a race of cavemen in Palestine in the patriarchal days. Now archeology has recovered these Horites, and they were not cave-dwellers. They were as advanced as anyone else of antiquity, and it is now known that Abraham had a thousand years of high culture behind him. The Horites are now called Hurrians. Excavation of the Mesopotamian town of Nuzi (1929) revealed legal and family customs. The Hurrian language is now taught in some universities.

Solomon

Solomon is fabled for his wisdom. However, ancient history is so silent about him that some scholars wondered if his wealth and wisdom were not exaggerated by the biblical records. However, several discoveries have greatly illustrated and confirmed the biblical picture, even though archeology has not discovered any tablets or inscriptions of Solomon. First, the town of Megiddo was excavated (1925-39). The buildings showed

Solomon's ability and interest in architecture. They verified his practice of establishing various chariot cities for defense (1 Kings 10:26). It is interesting to note that a six-pointed star is scratched on one of the slightly later buildings at Megiddo. This is the shield of David—which appears today on the flag of Israel. Later excavations in Hazor of Galilee (1955-59) show a similar prosperity in the Solomonic layer. The gateway at Hazor is said to be almost identical to the Solomonic gateway at Megiddo.

The researches south of the Dead Sea by Nelson Glueck are a further proof of Solomon's era. Glueck found several copper mines with crude smelting furnaces in the valley south of the Dead Sea. Pottery showed that the mines had been worked in the time of Solomon. Copper was evidently taken to Ezion-Geber (modern Eilat) on the eastern arm of the Red Sea. Glueck excavated a remarkable city in 1938, evidently planned and built as a unit and used for refining and casting copper and as a center of trade. The Bible says that Solomon's ships left Ezion-Geber for distant ports, bringing home rich cargoes (1 Kings 9:26-28). Archeology confirms the truth of the Bible. Solomon's ships exported copper and brought him rich revenue. He was a copper magnate of antiquity.

ANSWERING CRITICISM

The higher criticism carried on by liberal scholars has always been infused with skepticism. Though essentially an investigation of the Bible books' authorship and dates, it has had sad results for Christian teaching.

Higher criticism arose in a time of great ignorance of the Bible backgrounds. It assumed and taught that Palestine and Mesopotamia were as backward as Greece in 1500 B.C. It taught that Moses did not know how to write. The stories of the patriarchs were said to be the unbelievable and legendary folklore of the Hebrews of 900-700 B.C. They were *explanation stories*, like the Native American stories about how the bear lost its tail. Liberal critics said that the Genesis stories did nothing more than attempt to tell how family life began, why women hated snakes, and such.

Such error was difficult to answer in the days when the early history of the Near East was virtually unknown. Today such skepticism is foolish. It has been proven that in the days of Moses an educated man could write three or four languages. The patriarchs moved in a world of great powers and advanced cultures.

Of special importance are the advances that archeology has made in patriarchal backgrounds and in the Hebrew language. In 1929 the ancient town of Nuzi in Northern Mesopotamia was discovered. It yielded a wealth of tablets, generally dating back to about 1500 B.C. These illustrated the daily life and legal customs of the Hurrians and of the north Fertile Crescent. Outstanding archeologists—E. A. Speiser, W. F. Albright, and others—have shown how these customs support and explain even in detail many of the peculiar family customs of the patriarchs.

For example, Nuzi wedding contracts specify that if a wife is barren, she shall give a slave girl to her husband to provide a heir. Such a child shall have the right of a firstborn. But if the legal wife later bears a son, the earlier heir shall give way to him. These and many other customs exactly fit the patriarchal families. They do not fit the Israelite practices of 900-700 B.C. Some scholars have therefore become convinced of the historicity of the Genesis narrative.

It is most encouraging to see many of the citadels of liberalism so effectively overturned. Today even this newer liberalism is on the defensive. However, not all archeologists believe in verbal inspiration. Many things about the Old Testament cannot be proven by archeology. The Christian takes them on faith, trusting in the approval given them by Jesus Christ. At the same time, archeological discoveries have not required orthodox scholars to make any important revision in their viewpoint regarding the Bible's authenticity. It is reasonable to assume that further archeological study will give additional, welcome light and confirmation.

VOCABULARY ENRICHMENT

Archeology, cuneiform, Fertile Crescent, exicon, tablets, illumination.

DISCUSSION QUESTIONS

1. Give a brief history of archeology.
2. Give two examples of how archeology confirms the Bible.
3. Which came first, higher criticism or scientific archeology? What can be learned from this sequence?
4. Give an example of the way archeology has confounded higher criticism.
5. Use your concordance to list the references to the Horites.
6. Describe the archeological discoveries related to Solomon.
7. Examine at least one orthodox book on archeology.

11

HELPS FOR BIBLE STUDY

The best help for Bible study is the Bible itself. There is no substitute for a thorough knowledge of God's Word. Bible students should possess the best reference works and should give much thought to the edition of the Bible they are going to use.

The purpose and progress in Bible knowledge will influence greatly the decision as to what edition of the Bible to secure. Some people prefer a small Bible for ease in carrying. Others want a large-type Bible for ease in reading, especially in public reading. You should get a Bible that will last a reasonable length of time. When you become familiar with a Bible and have study notes in its margin, it is not easy to change.

You may want to get a Bible with thumb-notch indexes for the different books. Some like this feature; others do not. Anything that helps you to use your Bible conveniently and quickly is worth getting.

You probably will want a Bible with a concordance in the back if it does not make the Bible too bulky. A concordance lists and locates the words used in the Bible. An exhaustive concordance does this for every word in the Bible. An abridged concordance lists only the important words. It is the abridged concordance that is usually found in the back of many Bibles, and this tool is useful for quickly locating many verses.

REFERENCE BIBLES

Reference editions of the Bible are available from several publishers. Their notes or comments really constitute a brief commentary on the Bible. Such works are useful to the earnest, serious student. It is necessary, however, to distinguish carefully between what the Bible says and what the commentary notes say about the Bible. It is well to compare several commentaries or reference Bibles so as to understand various views. The *Scofield Reference* edition of the King James Version has been used by millions since its publication in 1908. It is now available in other versions.

The *Thompson Chain Reference Bible* has much material in the form of a concordance and Bible dictionary. It does not have the paragraph headings in the text but has them plainly marked in a wide margin. The wide margin itself is helpful for student notes. This edition also is available in several versions.

The Zondervan Publishing Company has also published a *New International Version Study Bible* with concordance and extensive explanatory notes, tables, and cross-references. The *Life Application Bible*, published by Tyndale House, is also a very helpful resource. Other good reference Bibles are also available.

TRANSLATIONS

Most important translations have been done by believing men. A few translations have been made by liberal scholars. Sometimes when translation is easy and the meaning is clear, this may make little difference. In other cases, when the meaning of the words is not so clear or where doctrinal matters are of importance, the liberals may allow their background to influence their translation. This is especially true in translations of the Old Testament prophecies of Christ.

King James or Authorized Version

This translation has been used for many years. Its translators were gifted scholars. They took time to do good quality work and were extremely conscientious and faithful. Its language may be slightly outmoded, and there are some modern discoveries that can be used to improve the translation here and there. But for general accuracy and time-honored beauty, it is still a favorite.

The *New King James Version* is a revision of the 1611 translation that uses more modern English forms and takes advantage of recently discovered manuscripts.

English Revised and American Standard Version

The English Revised Version of 1885 and American Standard Version of 1901 are also quite accurate. New Testament translators used more recently discovered Greek manuscripts and textual study in an attempt to improve upon earlier translations. These revised versions may seem somewhat stilted because the translators frequently used the Hebrew and Greek word order rather than the English. The result is that they do not have the excellent English of the King James Version. If the revisers had really brought the language up-to-date, the revision would be more acceptable for modern study. But their improvements are not of sufficient strength to overbalance their deficiencies.

Revised Standard Version

The *Revised Standard Version* reflects modern scholarship and presents some improvements. This was an ambitious work done over a long period. Unfortunately, many of the translators represented the modern critical position and did not believe all the truth of the Bible they were translating. Unless students can refer to the Hebrew and Greek, they do not know whether any particular verse is an accurate translation or not. Many times where the Hebrew is difficult, the translators decided that the text had become corrupt. In such cases they often changed the Hebrew text without manuscript evidence and then translated the supposed reading. Most of these places are marked in the footnotes as a "correction" (Cn.). The *New English Bible* did the same thing, marking such conjectures as the "probable reading."

The RSV translators seldom utilized any newly discovered text of the Old Testament. Whenever they have done so, they seem to have worked by conjecture or by unscientific use of the Septuagint or other old versions.

In recent years an updated version of the RSV, titled the *New Revised Standard Version Bible*, has appeared. The text has been carefully recast in fresh vocabulary and construction and reflects changes in the English language that have occurred since the original translation was published.

Even more recently a group of conservative evangelical scholars undertook a complete revision of the *Revised Standard Version*, seeking to correct the problems mentioned above. The Bible they have produced, titled the *English Standard Version*, is an essentially literal translation. It embraces the ideal of word-for-word exactness while at the same time taking into account the differences between modern English and the original languages. Translators sought the English words that most closely captured the meaning of the original. The result is a Bible that is both accurate and readable.

The *New English Bible* is the British counterpart of the *Revised Standard Version* in England, but the former is even more extreme. Again, the NEB is less reliable in the Old Testament. Actually the editors do not strictly translate. In many cases, they change the text in order to solve a difficulty. For instance, the psalm titles are omitted, and numerous passages in Job are dislocated. The *New English Bible* is beautifully written, modern in expression, and easy to read; however, its readings must be constantly checked for accuracy of translation and fidelity of text.

Other Translations

Several other translations are now available. They are of three kinds: liberal, conservative paraphrases, and conservative with strict principles of translation.

Of the first kind is the Roman Catholic *Jerusalem Bible*, which is liberal in its translation and extremely liberal in its extensive footnotes. The Roman Catholic *New American Bible* is much better in these regards. The *Good News Bible* is quite modern in expression and not fully conservative. For instance, it replaces references to the blood of Christ with references to His death. This alteration misses the Old Testament sacrificial connections.

A modern conservative paraphrase, *The Living Bible*, is very readable. However, it sometimes imparts a meaning to a verse that is not there. It should be compared with other versions for careful study. The *Amplified Bible* is somewhat different in that it offers several variant readings for particular words. It is interesting for private study, but difficult for general church use.

In the last category, several newer versions should be mentioned: the *New American Standard Bible*, the *New International Version*, and the *New Living Translation*. The *New American Standard Bible* is a careful, thorough revision of the *American Standard Version* done by competent evangelical scholars. Some think that this Bible is not done in the smoothest modern English. But it is accurate and faithful both to the text and to the spirit of the original. The *New International Version* was prepared by a large group of competent scholars. It is also true to the text, but gives a sentence-equivalence treatment rather than a word-for-word translation. The result is a smooth, highly readable translation suitable for study, reading, memorization, and public reading. It appears to be the most widely accepted version today. The *New Living Translation* is a thought-for-thought translation that can be readily understood by the average person. This translation adopts the vocabulary and language structures used by people today.

Your Library

Serious Christian workers need a library—at least a small library—and they should use it. Good leaders teach out of a fullness of material.

Effective teachers do not face their classes just a jump ahead of them in the manual.

Christian workers should have some books of a sound, popular nature on all the main divisions of Bible study. They need Bible dictionaries for technical helps, commentaries for explanation of hard passages, church histories for the study of the spread of the Gospel, books on Bible introduction for information on authorship and background, theology books for doctrinal study, and practical books for guidance in teaching, missions, and devotional life. The many evangelical publishers of our day should be patronized by Christians and their worthwhile books widely read.

A word of caution is in order. The study of liberal books may have a place for the well-grounded Christian. Their challenging statements may cause believers to rethink the basis of their faith and be ready to give an answer. New Christians or beginning students, however, cannot afford to give large place to these writers. Strychnine in small quantities is a stimulant. In larger amounts, it is deadly.

Commentaries

There is no one best commentary. For one purpose one commentary may excel; for another purpose, another. But the Bible student who has not had technical training will probably want one or two general purpose commentaries. For many years Matthew Henry; Jamieson, Fausset, and Brown; and Adam Clarke have been the favorites. These are valuable devotional commentaries and are still well accepted. The *New Bible Commentary: Revised* and the *Wycliffe Bible Commentary* are helpful. For more extensive study, the Tyndale Commentary series is good. For technical matters, the *New International Commentary* volumes can be consulted or *The Expositor's Bible Commentary*. Much newer information bearing on the Bible has been discovered in recent times, and these newer commentaries are worth consulting. Publication information about the above commentaries may be found in the Resources for Enrichment section at the end of this text.

Concordances

For those who need more help than the abridged concordance in the back of their Bible can provide, complete standard concordances are available. Two of these, Young's and Strong's, have about equal merit. In *Strong's Exhaustive Concordance*, every word is followed by a number. This number appears in the back of the book as a key to the original Hebrew or Greek word, transliterated in English letters.

STRONG'S CONCORDANCE

2051. וְדָן **Vᵉdân**, ved-awn'; perh. for 5730; *Vedan* (or Aden), a place in Arabia:—Dan also.

2052. וָהֵב **Vâhêb**, vaw-habe'; of uncert. der.; *Vaheb*, a place in Moab:—what he did.

2053. וָו **vâv**, vaw; prob. a *hook* (the name of the sixth Heb. letter):—hook.

2054. וָזָר **vâzâr**, vaw-zawr'; presumed to be from an unused root mean. to *bear* guilt: crime:— × strange.

2055. וַיְזָתָא **Vayᵉzâthâ'**, vah-yez-aw'-thaw; of for. or.; *Vajezatha*, a son of Haman:—Vajezatha.

2056. וָלָד **vâlâd**, vaw-lawd'; for 3206; a *boy*:—child

2057. וַנְיָה **Vanyâh**, van-yaw'; perh. for 6043; *Vaniah*, an Isr.:—Vaniah.

2058. וָפְסִי **Vophçiy**, vof-see'; prob. from 3254; *additional*; *Vophsi*, an Isr.:—Vophsi.

2059. וַשְׁנִי **Vashniy**, vash-nee'; prob. from 3161: *weak*; *Vashni*, an Isr.:—Vashni.

2060. וַשְׁתִּי **Vashtiy**, vash-tee'; of Pers. or.; *Vashti*, the queen of Xerxes:—Vashti.

child ^ See also CHILDBEARING; CHILDHOOD; CHILDLESS; CHILDREN; CHILD'S.

Ge	11:30 Sarai was barren; she had no c'.	2056
	16:11 her, Behold, thou art with c',	2030
	17:10 Every man c' among you shall	*
	12 every man c' in your generations,*	
	14 the uncircumcised man c' whose*	
	19:36 both the daughters of Lot with c'	2030
	21: 8 the c' grew, and was weaned:	3206
	14 and the c', and sent her away:	
	15 cast the c' under one of the shrubs."	
	16 Let me not see the death of the c'.	"
	37:30 The c' is not; and I, whither shall	"
	38:24 she is with c' by whoredom.	2030
	25 am I with c': and she said,	"
	42:22 Do not sin against the c';	3206
	44:20 and a c' of his old age, a little one;	"
Ex	2: 2 saw him that he was a goodly c',	
	3 and put the c' therein; and she	3206
	6 had opened it, she saw the c':	"
	7 women, that she may nurse the c'	"
	9 Take this c' away, and nurse it	"
	9 the woman took the c', and nursed	"
	10 and the c' grew, and she brought	"
	21:22 hurt a woman with c', so that her	2030
	22:22 afflict any widow, or fatherless c'.	

In *Young's Analytical Concordance to the Bible*, the Hebrew or Greek word is printed with the English word. A section at the back tells what English words are used to translate each original word. For instance, you can look up the word *paidia*, "child," and find that it is translated twenty-five times "child," four times "damsel," twelve times "little child," and ten times "young child." These English words give a complete picture of the Greek word. This is no substitute for actually reading the Greek or Hebrew, but this tool is a great help. A Hebrew dictionary that can be used by nontechnical students is the *Theological Wordbook of the Old Testament*. Since its entries are keyed to Strong's *Concordance*, it can be used in a limited way by those with little or no Hebrew.

Bible Dictionary

Do you want to know how a word is used or what it means? What is a pomegranate, a farthing, a cherub? How old is Jerusalem? Where is Ai? A Bible dictionary or encyclopedia gives the answers to questions such as these.

In this field the *International Standard Bible Encyclopedia* has been the standard for many years among orthodox scholars. A similar work is Merrill Tenney's five-volume *The Zondervan Pictorial Encyclopedia of the Bible*. Less exhaustive but very suitable is the one-volume *The Zondervan Pictorial Bible Dictionary* by the same editor. J. D. Douglas's *New Bible Dictionary* also is valuable, as is the *Wycliffe Bible Encyclopedia*. Charles Pfeiffer has a general reference dictionary on archeology, *The Biblical World*. See the Resources for Enrichment section for further information about these resources.

Bible Introduction

Who wrote Judges? When did Paul visit Rome? When was the Old Testament canon closed? Which Gospel was written first? Bible dictionaries and encyclopedias give partial answers. Books on Bible introduction have more complete, satisfactory answers to these questions.

Some books deal with specialized or limited subjects. Some are technical, but Christian students should not be afraid of a little study. In this field as in some others, however, it is wise to avoid books tainted with liberalism, since they do not usually present all the evidence. This leaves students with a half truth that is dangerous, especially if they are not able to study further. In the New Testament field, the *Introduction to the New Testament* by Thiessen is a standard. The Old Testament field is more technical. Unger's *Introductory Guide to the Old Testament* may be valuable. The writer's own book, *Inspiration and Canonicity of the Bible*, and *Survey of Old Testament Introduction* by Gleason L. Archer, Jr., deal with some of these subjects in a more popular way. O. T. Allis's *The Five Books of Moses* is standard for discussion of the Pentateuch.

Theology Books

Benjamin B. Warfield, great theologian of the past generation, said, "The best theological professor is a Christian mother." Every Christian mother should work faithfully at her teacher's task. At an early age the author was taught a complete system of theology by his mother. She made him memorize the Westminster Shorter Catechism. Actually such creeds as the Westminster Confession of Faith and Catechisms, the Heidelberg Catechism, and the Lutheran Augsburg Confession are theology textbooks in a small yet vital compass.

A readable work on theology is by Dr. J. Oliver Buswell, Jr., *A Systematic Theology of the Christian Religion*. An excellent short study on theology is *In Understanding Be Men* by T. C. Hammond of England. It has a scriptural, popular approach. Widely used and good are *Basic Christianity* by John R. W. Stott and *Mere Christianity* by C. S. Lewis. An older book by A. A. Hodge, *Outlines of Theology*, also deserves careful study. There are many other well-written, conservative texts in theology; so students need not feel limited in their study.

Miscellaneous Reading and Study

Have you read any church history? It is fascinating. Try F. F. Bruce's *The Spreading Flame*. This is the first in a series of popular books on the history of the church. Earle E. Cairns's *Christianity Through the*

Centuries covers the whole field in one volume. How many biographies have you read? The stories of D. L. Moody, Charles Hadden Spurgeon, Morrison of China, Judson of Burma, William Carey of India, Hudson Taylor of China, George Mueller of England, and many others are fascinating reading. Many books are available on modern experiences, such as Corrie Ten Boom's *The Hiding Place*, or on modern problems, such as Francis Schaeffer's *Escape from Reason*. And then there are the widely known books of C. S. Lewis on many subjects. Fill your life with such literature.

VOCABULARY ENRICHMENT

Bible introduction, commentary, concordance, reference Bible.

DISCUSSION QUESTIONS

1. Compare the translation of Hebrews 1 in the King James Version, the *New International Version*, the *American Standard Version*, and the *Revised Standard Version*.
2. Do the same for Psalm 45.
3. Evaluate the merits and weaknesses of the King James Version, the *New International Version*, the *American Standard Version*, and the *Revised Standard Version*. Explain your position.
4. Trace in Young's or Strong's concordance the uses of the Hebrew word *tsur*, "rock." (There are seventy-six usages, with the Hebrew translated by nine English words or phrases.) In how many of these is God called a rock?
5. Use a Bible dictionary or encyclopedia to look up the dates of the reign of Sargon, king of Assyria, and tell something about him.
6. Try to find five of the books mentioned in this chapter. Do you have any of these in your own library? If not, your pastor may let you check his library. What about your church or Sunday school library?

12

BIBLE STUDY METHODS

"How can I improve my knowledge of the Bible?" "How can I really study and understand God's Word?" These companion questions are frequently asked by serious-minded Christians. They deserve careful thought because the contents of the Bible are so varied, and the backgrounds are so different. The study of God's Word has occupied many people of great ability through the centuries. How can you unlock its treasures?

Two things must be considered—how to appreciate and understand the Bible better and how to get more of the Bible's blessing for daily living. The first concerns Bible study; the other is related to devotional life. Unfortunately, it is possible to have one without the other. The well-taught, well-balanced Christian understands the Word of God and takes it to heart.

DEVOTIONAL READING

Nothing can substitute for daily reading of the Bible. It should be devotional reading—prayerful, thoughtful reading with a prepared heart. All kinds of devotional helps are available today. And certainly everyone agrees that the Holy Spirit is the great Teacher.

For devotions, do not read too much at a time. It is better to cover half a chapter, underlining the striking verses and jotting down the lessons learned, than to read hurriedly through three chapters without taking any of it to heart. Though it takes time and discipline, it is a good practice to memorize verses and chapters. These should be reviewed frequently and shared with others.

Some portions are well adapted to devotional reading. Others, like the genealogies and laws of cleanliness, do not adapt to devotional reading, even though they are true and important.

New Christians will find it helpful to begin devotional reading by using the Psalms or the four Gospels, especially John. The Acts and the shorter Epistles are helpful. But wherever people begin, they should keep their hearts open for God's blessing.

A word of caution may be said on devotional helps. Numerous devotional books and quarterlies have been written by liberal authors. Some have the idea that quietness, emotionalism, and stained-glass windows are the essence of devotion. If so, Paul had a meager devotional life. A pamphlet that quotes a verse of Scripture out of context and tells a story about a little boy who gave his allowance to his brother and closes with a prayer, "O Lord, help us to help one another," is no help to devotion.

Does your devotional guide exalt the Lord Jesus Christ as the supernatural, miracle-working, sin-bearing, resurrected Savior? Does it encourage you to seek positive answers to prevailing prayer? Does it offer the meat of the Word adequately interpreted? If not, scrutinize it again. Choose from the many sound books, such as *Daily Light, My Utmost for His Highest,* and *Streams in the Desert.* Biblically sound radio and TV devotional programs also are helpful.

BIBLE STUDY

Christian workers need more than devotional reading of the Bible. Teachers and leaders especially need to know the facts, doctrines, and backgrounds of the Bible. Without thorough Bible knowledge, they will not be able to answer the questions of others or to bring out the rich truths of the Word.

How shall we study the Bible and master it? Any answer implies a willingness to study. Mathematics, French, and chemistry are not learned without application. This is equally true of the Bible.

Bible study involves the use of books written by Bible scholars. Why? The early Christians did not debate extensively the meanings of the Epistles. They knew the language and the backgrounds of the writings. Today most Christian workers do not know either Greek or Hebrew. Nor do they have a broad, general knowledge of ancient times. So they must depend on those who do know this information. It is, therefore, important to use such studies intelligently. In a fundamental seminary or Bible college, the Bible is studied from a variety of angles. Most teachers, workers, or officers of the local church have not had such formal training, but they can study the Bible diligently and consistently.

Dr. Wilbur M. Smith, in his useful book *Profitable Bible Study,* advocates several methods of approach—a book at a time (often too much for a beginner), studying by chapters, by paragraphs, by verses, and by words. He suggests the study of Bible biographies and prayers and reminds us that all the material should be related to Christ and His work for us. He quotes Miss Grace Saxe's ten questions to ask of each chapter:

What is the leading subject?
What is the leading lesson?
What is the best verse?
Who is the principal person?
What does it teach of Christ?
Does it show an example to follow?
Is there any error to avoid?
Is there a duty to perform?
Does it give a promise to claim?
Is there a prayer to echo?

Dr. Smith quotes Dr. Howard A. Kelly, famous Christian surgeon of Baltimore, who said that "the greatest secret of Bible study is simply to do it!"

What appears to a beginner as a great knowledge of the Bible is thus often only the natural result of a persevering use of the simplest of all methods—namely, reading the book day by day until it becomes extremely familiar in all its parts.

Bible Book Study

Study of the books or portions is called exegesis or interpretation. Several steps lead to success in this type of study. First, the book should be read many times. Then an outline should be made to analyze the book. The general contents should be placed in plain view, showing the relationship of each part to every other. It will be of help to ask these questions.

Does the book have a main theme?
How is the theme developed?
If the book is historical, what is the historian's viewpoint?
What does the author emphasize?

In some books, such as the Psalms, the themes are not easily unified. Such a book should be studied by individual units.

Literary Division

You may want to study a verse at a time or to treasure certain verses apart from context. Louis M. Sweet's *The Study of the English Bible* is a healthy protest against this piecemeal approach. Sweet's book follows the method of Dr. W. W. White, that of observing the literary units of paragraphs and larger wholes. Many Bibles have the paragraphs or literary units marked. The natural division should be carefully kept in mind in study.

Bible Introduction

It is important to know the background of each book and the reason for its writing. A good book on Bible introduction will provide this information. For instance, in the study of Colossians, you will discover that this book is one of four Prison Epistles written by Paul from Rome. This fact explains the agreement between Ephesians and Colossians—a similarity so striking that the one helps to explain the other. Both were written against a background of the growing heresy of Gnosticism. Therefore, Paul emphasized the uniqueness of Christ. This background information enriches your interpretation. An extensive study of history and archeology will also help in attaining the goal of increased Bible knowledge.

Doctrinal Study

This study, known as systematic theology, can be as exhaustive as your time and ability will allow. Doctrinal study strengthens interpretation, and correct interpretation is necessary for doctrinal study.

A study of "Christ" in Hebrews 1 shows the error of the claim of some liberal theologians that Colossians 1:15 teaches that Christ is firstborn among equals. Rather it reveals Him as the unique Son of God who existed before any of the things that He Himself created. Comparison of Scripture with Scripture is proper and profitable because the Holy Spirit is the Author of it all. He directs and guides as you trace each doctrine through the entire book.

Careful study of "Christ in the Prison Epistles" will uncover truths usually missed in general book study. Doctrinal study has a stabilizing influence and helps produce virile Christians.

It may be difficult to remember all the texts bearing on "the nature of sin," but a brief doctrinal statement from a catechism or a book on systematic theology will summarize the Bible's teaching on this subject. This is useful in Christian life as well as in Christian study.

Historical Study

Another fruitful method of study is by historical periods. This is important in the Old Testament where the books are not arranged chronologically. Companion books should be studied together. The following grouping will help.

Old Testament

The Pentateuch (Genesis-Deuteronomy) is a unit and concerns the early times.

The psalms of David go with the books of Samuel.

Proverbs, Ecclesiastes, and the Song of Solomon fit in with the early chapters of 1 Kings.

Isaiah should be read with the first six Minor Prophets—Hosea, Joel, Amos, Obadiah, Jonah, and Micah.

Jeremiah, Ezekiel, Daniel, and the three Minor Prophets—Nahum, Habakkuk, and Zephaniah—are approximately of the same time period.

Ezra, Nehemiah, and the last three Minor Prophets are of the post-exilic times.

Passages in 2 Samuel should be read and compared with 1 Chronicles to see if they are parallel or supplementary passages.

Likewise, 2 Chronicles should be compared with 1 Kings and 2 Kings.

New Testament

In the New Testament the time span is shorter, but the historical background is equally important. An interesting way to study Acts would be to stop at each place where Paul wrote an epistle. Before continuing, read the corresponding epistle. This method interweaves the book of Acts and the Pauline Epistles, enriching the interpretation.

Word Study

The aim of all exegesis is simply to find out what the Bible says. When we read magazines or newspapers, we do not have to engage in exegesis because we are thoroughly familiar with the language. Occasionally we meet a strange word, and then we consult a dictionary. In reading more difficult material, we use exegesis more.

The Bible was written in Greek, Hebrew, and Aramaic. These are strange languages to us, and the customs of antiquity are unfamiliar or perhaps unknown. The biblical material concerns deep and wonderful divine truths. Therefore, we must probe deeply into the meaning of the Bible's text. Word study is often helpful in this process. This investigation of a word's usage and derivation involves the use of dictionaries and other reference books.

For instance, Jesus said, "I am the bread of life" (John 6:35). What did He mean? Is Jesus bread? How do "bread" and "life" fit together?

Here is deeper truth to be gained by study. For such word study, look up all Jesus' references to bread, especially to His being bread. He evidently was not talking about physical life or physical bread. Notice that Christ also claims to give the "light of life" (John 8:12) and the "living water" (John 7:38). Study the other metaphors using the expression, "I am"—"I am the door" (John 10:9); "I am the way, the truth, and the life" (John 14:6). Word study will bring out the deeper truths.

Some words are strange to us. A much debated word is *baptize*. Word study will not provide an absolutely final answer. If it did, all discussion would cease. But you should look up all the uses of this word. Whatever your view, you should investigate the biblical data. Take Young's or Strong's concordance, find how many ways the Greek word *baptizo* is translated. Check all these references. Your investigation of the evidence will enable you to make sure your view is based on facts. Word study is a valuable tool in exegesis.

Combinations of Bible Study Methods

All methods of Bible study are interrelated. You do not learn all the doctrines before you begin exegesis. Nor do you study a whole book and its component paragraphs before you investigate its background. The fact is, all methods should be used at all times. No one should use book study or the verse-by-verse method of interpretation without using the others. Conscientious students who use supplementary materials will improve their personal lives and ministry. A major purpose of this course has been to give guidance and suggestions in this further Bible study. Full-orbed Bible study is a blessing.

"Blessed is he that readeth, and they that hear the words of this prophecy, and keep those things which are written therein; for the time is at hand" (Rev. 1:3).

VOCABULARY ENRICHMENT

Catechism, chronology, doctrinal study, exegesis, Gnosticism, historical study, interpretation, systematic theology, textual study, word study.

DISCUSSION QUESTIONS

1. Give two reasons why New Testament exegesis is more of a problem today than it was for the early Christian church.
2. Why should Christians study the Bible both devotionally and technically?

3. What information would a close study of an epistle such as 2 Timothy reveal about what time in Paul's life and under what circumstances it was written?

4. Using the Westminster Shorter Catechism, Heidelberg Catechism, or any other catechism, look up the doctrine of the person of Christ. ·

5. Describe the Bible study methods you have used.

NOTES

1 REVELATION AND INSPIRATION

1. C. S. Lewis, *Miracles* (New York: Macmillan, 1947), p. 74.

2. E. D. Hirsch, *The Aims of Interpretation* (Chicago: University of Chicago, 1976), p. 41.

3. Norman L. Geisler, ed., *Inerrancy* (Grand Rapids: Zondervan Publishing, 1980), chapters 12, 13.

5 WHO WROTE THE NEW TESTAMENT?

1. Cited and defended by Donald Guthrie, *New Testament Introduction*, Vol. 3 (Downers Grove, Ill.: InterVarsity Press, 1965), pp. 321-22.

2. Quoted by Eusebius in his *Ecclesiastical History*, vi, 25.

3. Alexander Roberts and James Donaldson, eds., *Early Church Fathers, The Ante-Nicene Fathers*, Vol. 4 (Hendrickson, Mass.: 1994), pp. 310, 333, 361ff.

4. Ibid., p. 388.

7 PRESERVATION OF THE BIBLE: OLD TESTAMENT

1. See the article "Nergal-sharezer" by E. M. Yamauchi in *Wycliffe Bible Encyclopedia*, ed. Charles F. Pfeiffer, H. F. Vos, and J. Rea (Chicago: Moody Press, 1975).

9 HIGHER CRITICISM AND THE BIBLE

1. Martin Noth, *A History of Pentateuchal Traditions*, tr. B. W. Anderson (Chico, Calif.: Scholars Press, 1981), pp. 17-18.

RESOURCES FOR ENRICHMENT

Albright, William F. "Recent Discoveries in Bible Lands." Supplement of *Young's Analytical Concordance to the Bible*. Rev. ed. Grand Rapids: Wm. B. Eerdmans Publishing, 1955.

Allis, Oswald T. *The Five Books of Moses*. Grand Rapids: Baker Book House, 1977.

_____. *The Unity of Isaiah*. Grand Rapids: Baker Book House, n.d.

Archer, Gleason L., Jr. *A Survey of Old Testament Introduction*. Rev. ed. Chicago: Moody Press, 1973.

_____. *Encyclopedia of Bible Difficulties*. Grand Rapids: Zondervan Publishing, 1982.

Bruce, F. F. *The New Testament Documents: Are They Reliable?* 5th rev. ed. Grand Rapids: Wm. B. Eerdmans Publishing, 1960.

_____. *The Spreading Flame*. Grand Rapids: Wm. B. Eerdmans Publishing, 1980.

_____. *New International Commentary on the New Testament*. Grand Rapids: Wm. B. Eerdmans Publishing, 1994.

Buswell, J. Oliver, Jr. *A Systematic Theology of the Christian Religion*. Grand Rapids: Zondervan Publishing, 1962.

Cairns, Earle E. *Christianity Through the Centuries*. Grand Rapids: Zondervan Publishing, 1967.

Carson, D. A., and Woodbridge, John D., eds. *Scripture and Truth*. Grand Rapids: Zondervan Publishing, 1983.

Douglas, J. D., ed. *The New Bible Dictionary*. Grand Rapids: Wm. B. Eerdmans Publishing, 1962.

Finegan, Jack. *Light from the Ancient Past: The Archaeological Background of Judaism and Christianity*. 2nd ed. 2 vols. Princeton, N.J.: Princeton University Press, 1970.

Gaebelein, F. *The Expositor's Bible Commentary*. Grand Rapids: Zondervan Publishing, 1979.

Geisler, Norman L., ed. *Inerrancy*. Grand Rapids: Zondervan Publishing, 1980.

Geisler, Norman, L., and Nix, William E. *From God to Us: How We Got Our Bible.* Chicago: Moody Press, 1974.

Gish, Duane T. *Evolution: The Challenge of the Fossil Record.* El Cajon, Calif.: Creation-Life Publishers, 1985.

Greenlee, J. H. "Text and Manuscripts of the New Testament." *The Zondervan Pictorial Encyclopedia of the Bible.* 5 vols. Ed. Merrill C. Tenney. Grand Rapids: Zondervan Publishing, 1975.

Guthrie, Donald. "Canon of the New Testament." In vol. 1 of *The Zondervan Pictorial Encyclopedia of the Bible.* 5 vols. Ed. Merrill C. Tenney. Grand Rapids: Zondervan Publishing, 1975.

_____. *New Testament Introduction.* 3 vols. Chicago: InterVarsity Press, 1965.

Guthrie, Donald, and Motyer, J. A., eds. *The New Bible Commentary: Revised.* Grand Rapids: Wm. B. Eerdmans Publishing, 1970.

Haley, J. W. *An Examination of the Alleged Discrepancies of the Bible.* Nashville: B. C. Goodpasture, 1958.

Hammond, T. C. *In Understanding Be Men.* London: InterVarsity Press, 1936.

Harris, R. Laird. "Canon of the Old Testament." In vol. 1 of *The Zondervan Pictorial Encyclopedia of the Bible.* 5 vols. Ed. Merrill C. Tenney. Grand Rapids: Zondervan Publishing, 1975.

_____. *Inspiration and Canonicity of the Bible.* Rev. ed. Grand Rapids: Zondervan Publishing, 1969.

_____, ed. *Theological Wordbook of the Old Testament.* Chicago: Moody Press, 1980.

Harrison, R. K. "Dead Sea Scrolls." In vol. 2 of *The Zondervan Pictorial Encyclopedia of the Bible.* 5 vols. Ed. Merrill C. Tenney. Grand Rapids: Zondervan Publishing, 1975.

_____, ed. *New International Commentary on the Old Testament.* Grand Rapids: Wm. B. Eerdmans Publishing.

Helm, Paul. *The Divine Revelation.* Chicago: Good News Publishers, 1982.

Jensen, Irving L. *Enjoy Your Bible.* Chicago: Moody Press, 1969.

Lewis, C. S. *Mere Christianity.* New York: Macmillan Co., 1960.

_____. *Miracles, A Preliminary Study.* New York: Macmillan Co., 1947.

Orr, James, ed. *The International Standard Bible Encyclopedia.* Chicago: Howard Severance Co., 1930.

Parker, Gary. *Creation, the Facts of Life*. El Cajon, Calif.: Creation-Life Publishers, 1980.

Perry, Lloyd M., and Culver, Robert D. *How to Get More from Your Bible*. Grand Rapids: Baker Book House, 1979.

Pfeiffer, Charles F. *Dead Sea Scrolls and the Bible*. Grand Rapids: Baker Book House, 1969.

_____, ed. *The Biblical World, a Dictionary of Biblical Archaeology*. Grand Rapids: Baker Book House, 1966.

Pfeiffer, Charles F., and Harrison, E. F., eds. *The Wycliffe Bible Commentary*. Chicago: Moody Press, 1962.

Pfeiffer, Charles F., and Vos, H. F., eds. *Wycliffe Bible Encyclopedia*. 2 vols. Chicago: Moody Press, 1975.

Pun, Pattle P. T. *Evolution: Nature and Scripture in Conflict?* Grand Rapids: Zondervan Publishing, 1982.

Schaeffer, Francis A. *Escape from Reason*. Downers Grove, Ill.: InterVarsity Press, 1979.

Scroggie, W. Graham. *A Guide to the Gospels*. Old Tappan, N.J.: Fleming H. Revell, 1975.

Sproul, R. C. "The Case for Inerrancy." *God's Inerrant Word*. Ed. J. W. Mungor. Minneapolis: Bethany Fellowship, 1974.

Stott, John R. W. *Basic Christianity*. Grand Rapids: Wm. B. Eerdmans Publishing, 1957.

Tasker, R. V. G., ed. *Tyndale New Testament Commentary*. Grand Rapids: Wm. B. Eerdmans Publishing, 1979.

Ten Boom, Corrie. *The Hiding Place*. Minneapolis: Billy Graham Assn., 1971.

Tenney, Merrill C. *New Testament Survey*. Rev. ed. Grand Rapids: Wm. B. Eerdmans Publishing, 1961.

_____, ed. *The Zondervan Pictorial Bible Dictionary*. Grand Rapids: Zondervan Publishing, 1967.

Thiessen, Henry C. *Introduction to the New Testament*. Grand Rapids: Wm. B. Eerdmans Publishing, 1971.

Thompson, J. A. *The Bible and Archeology*. Rev. ed. Grand Rapids: Wm. B. Eerdmans Publishing, 1981.

Unger, Merrill F. *Archeology and the Old Testament*. Grand Rapids: Zondervan Publishing, 1954.

_____. *Introductory Guide to the Old Testament*. Grand Rapids: Zondervan Publishing, 1951.

Vos, Howard. *Effective Bible Study*. Grand Rapids: Zondervan Publishing, 1956.

Wald, Oletta. *The Joy of Discovery in Bible Study*. Minneapolis: Augsburg Publishing House, 1975.

Warfield, B. B. *The Inspiration and Authority of the Bible*. Nutley, N.J.: Presbyterian and Reformed Publishing, 1948.

Wenham, J. W., "Christ's View of Scripture," and Blum, E. P., "The Apostles' View of Scripture." *Inerrancy*. Ed. Norman L. Geisler. Grand Rapids: Zondervan Publishing, 1980.

Wiseman, D. J., ed. *Tyndale Old Testament Commentaries*. Chicago: InterVarsity Press.

Young, Edward J. *An Introduction to the Old Testament*. Grand Rapids: Wm. B. Eerdmans Publishing, 1958.

Since 1930

Evangelical Training Association

THE MINISTRIES OF EVANGELICAL TRAINING ASSOCIATION (ETA)

Experienced – Founded in 1930.

Doctrinally Dependable – Conservative and evangelical theology.

Educationally Sound – Engaging all adult learning styles.

Thoroughly Field-Tested – Used by a global constituency.

Recommended – Officially endorsed by denominations and schools.

Ministry Driven – Committed to quality training resources for equipping lay volunteers to serve Christ more effectively in the church.

Affordable – Attractive and reasonably priced.

For many local ministries, the most important step to an effective lay leadership training program is locating and implementing an inspiring, motivational system of instruction. ETA curriculum is available as traditional classroom courses, audio and video seminars, audio and video CD-ROM packages, and other resources for your classroom teaching or personal study.

Contact ETA today for free information and a 20-minute video presentation. Request Information Packet: Crossway Partner.

EVANGELICAL TRAINING ASSOCIATION
110 Bridge Street • PO Box 327 • Wheaton, IL 60189
800-369-8291 • FAX 630-668-8437 • www.etaworld.org